W. L. Greene

Worth Keeping

Selected from the Congregationalist and Boston Recorder, 1870-1879

W. L. Greene

Worth Keeping
Selected from the Congregationalist and Boston Recorder, 1870-1879

ISBN/EAN: 9783337232757

Printed in Europe, USA, Canada, Australia, Japan

Cover: Foto ©Suzi / pixelio.de

More available books at **www.hansebooks.com**

"The great billows instantly flooded and submerged her."　　Page 10.

WORTH KEEPING:

SELECTED FROM

The Congregationalist and Boston Recorder,

1870–1879.

BOSTON:

W. L. GREENE & CO.

CONGREGATIONAL HOUSE,

CORNER BEACON AND SOMERSET STREETS,

1880.

PREFACE.

Such has been the success of the two previous volumes made up of articles from the *Congregationalist* ("Household Reading," issued in 1866, and "Good Things," in 1870), as to show that there is a general desire to possess in a more permanent form than the newspaper page sketches, essays and poems that have attracted special attention at the time of their publication. With this idea in mind "Worth Keeping" has been selected as the name for this volume; and, like "Good Things," its contents will be found appropriate for the Sabbath school library. The writers are among the most valued contributors to the *Congregationalist*, and such articles have been selected as will not be likely to lie upon the library shelves unused.

The book is designed for family reading, and while but few of its chapters can be classed properly as juvenile, most of them are such as may be expected to interest young people as well as those of a more mature age.

Being fragmentary in its contents, the book has the advantage of great variety, and of articles from many different writers, thus possessing especial attractiveness as a book to lie upon the center table for use in odd minutes and for a spare half hour.

A fair idea may be gathered from its pages of the general character, scope and value of the *Congregationalist*, considered especially as a family religious newspaper.

CONTENTS.

PROSE.

POETRY.

OUTRIDING A CYCLONE AT SEA.

ETURNING from Europe in September, 1875, our steamship was struck in mid-ocean at daybreak by a cyclone. The sea had been vexed by autumn gales, and the waves contrary for some days. But this black angel spread his wings on the water without warning. A cyclone moves with the stealth and spring of a panther. The shock was sudden, tremendous, awful. The blast of the tempest, riding the gulf stream all the way from the heated tropics, was like the breath of a fiery furnace. It was the same cyclone which damaged Galveston, and tearing through the Gulf of Mexico, swept up the Atlantic coast and out upon the ocean, spreading wreck and death.

Our iron ship was stanch and well manned, but the first swirl of the whirlwind, traveling in its might like a majestic cylinder of fire-storm, stripped a portion of the guards and boats from the deck, and carried one of the crew into the sea, breaking his leg. He caught a stray rope and was rescued. The man at the wheel lost control of the vessel for a little, and veering round, she went into the trough of the sea. The great billows instantly flooded and submerged her, and the sea-water poured down the hatchway and through the sky-lights on the deck like falls of a mill-dam. Those in the saloon, feeling the roll of the ship, the waves going over her, and seeing the green water starred with foam at the port-holes, and in the descending cataract within, threatening to fill every room and cabin in the ship, will never forget the scene. This was repeated several times. The wind blew so fiercely that the waves were cut off completely by it, and leveled like a floor, and the foam made it look white and fleecy, like wool spread out upon a plain.

The ship could not be guided into the teeth of the wind at right angles with the waves, but must be made to "quarter on," striking each wave at an angle of forty-five degrees. In this way there was a constant strain on the machinery, tending to force the ship round parallel with the waves, so she would roll helplessly in the trough of the sea, and soon go to pieces. The trial of her strength in this way, hour after hour, was fearfully great. When the stern would be down in the water, and the prow climbing a wave, the cut of the iron ship upon it sounded as if it were grating on the side of a vast granite rock, making the whole ship tremble as she labored staggeringly over it. Then, in going down on the other side, the stern of the ship would be lifted from the water, and the increased speed of

the great propelling screw, freed from the resist-
ance of the water and driven by the force of a
thousand horse power, would shake and jar the
ship as if it were coming to pieces. The passengers assembled in the dining-saloon and clung to
tables and sofas and chairs round the room, which
were chained to the floor. It was impossible to
walk, or sit, or recline, without holding on to some
object with great firmness. Many were thrown
and tossed about like footballs, and much injured.
For eighteen hours this stress of weather was on
us. For eighteen hours, with few interruptions, I
sat on the edge of a sofa, clinging to a table before
me; my wife lying on the sofa, and I bracing back
against her so as to keep her from being thrown
upon the floor. It was a severe test of physical
endurance. The sun rose and found us there; it
set and left us there. It was not until near midnight that the winds began to abate. Then for
hours the sickening roll of the retiring waves was
very trying in our state of exhaustion. It was a
long time to endure hardness.

After the danger of the first shock was passed,
the ship's power to resist before it must give way
was only a question of time. Strained to the
utmost in every part, the time was coming when it
must weaken somewhere. Neither could the brave
and faithful men who manned her long hold out.
Any moment some seam might open in the ship,
some part of the toiling machinery break, and all

be over. The sea was lashed into fury in its hights
and depths. Death sat on the floods. Peril looked
in at the windows. The roar and tumult was terrific. We were 1,500 miles from shore each way.
There was but a plank between us and eternity.

For the first fifteen minutes, when death seemed
inevitable, my shrinking and recoil from death was
very strong. It was a terror to think of being cast
into such an angry, surging sea. Then came the
thought, I cannot give up my work for Christ now;
His service is a joy, and in my strength I want to
live and toil for Him. After this came thoughts
of my children and friends, and my church in St.
Louis. I said in my heart, my work is not done.
I cannot part with them now. Lord, spare me
from this hour. When this tide of thought and
emotion had swept swiftly past, it was as if Jesus
came to me walking on the sea. My heart leaped
out to Him in complete assurance and rest. "Perfect love casteth out fear." From that moment He
was my refuge, and all burden went. There was a
great calm in my soul. Heaven seemed near and
unutterably precious. The bright way to it through
the crystal waters appeared short and beautiful as
a pavement of emerald. There was a feeling of
resignation and readiness, then and there, in the
midst of the boiling, tempestuous sea, to go home
to the Heavenly Father's house. From that early
point to the end, I was permitted to minister to
others.

The occasion required a soul calm and serene and confident in God. The crash of the sea and the revels of the wind, and the thunder of the far deep were mingled with the shrieks and groans of the affrighted passengers. Under the influence of fear the eyes protruded as in strangulation and drowning. All classes were in prayer, asking mercy and seeking piteously to be directed. The interest in personal salvation was instant and universal. A Jew sat at my feet fifteen hours, leaving only at the briefest intervals. The group around me, clinging to their holds, listened to the words of salvation as for their lives. The Bible seemed builded as an armory wherein hung a thousand promises, all mighty shields for men in the perils of the sea. The Old Volume and the New, Christ and the Apostles, all spake for "those who go down to the sea in ships and do business in great waters."

Every few minutes I tore a blank leaf from my note-book, and my wife, as I steadied her, writing down some wonderful promise of God, the paper was passed round the whole circle from hand to hand, and read with intense interest and comfort, each one in turn looking up at the writer with a glance of grateful recognition. Some of the passages will readily recur to the reader :

When thou passest through the waters, I will be with thee; and through the rivers, they shall not overflow thee. *Is. xliii : 2.*

He commandeth and raiseth the stormy wind. Their

soul is melted because of trouble.   Then they cry unto the
Lord in their trouble, and he bringeth them out of their distresses.   *Ps. cvii : 25–28.*

At length God lifted his frown from the sea and
visited us with His smile. " He maketh the storm
a calm.   So that the waves thereof are still."   On
the Sabbath that followed, praise and gratitude to
God rose in the worship like incense.   There were
no dry eyes or indifferent hearts.   Many who had
been the most reckless in their excesses and pro-
fanity, said : "Our prayers and our trust in Christ,
commenced in storm, shall never cease in calm."

The experience was of great value. I know now
how it will seem to die.   It is going home in the
light and peace of Christ.   I know the keeping
power of our Lord in the hour of mortal terror and
fear.   I know the might of His arm to uplift and
cheer the soul in its extremities.   I know the
wondrous sweetness of His grace and love when
human strength fails.   I know that the near
approaches to Him are like sunrise to the soul,
and that the entrance ways to His presence chamber, through one of which I glanced, are filled with
the brightness of the King's countenance and the
gleam of angelic hosts.   When the gates of light
swing before us, and we enter into the joy of our
Lord, it will be a moment of supreme inspiration
and gladness.   Since that day when God hid me in
his pavilion and taught me, I have been, I trust, a
better guide to souls in need, in the house of prayer,

and in the chambers of pain and suffering. I asked for the redemption of a hundred souls that year. I record it to the praise of God that He gave that number and more.

There is a cleft in the rock for refuge from the frenzy of the storm, and hidden manna for the soul. We can say with Christ, "I have meat to eat that ye know not of."

"ONLY ME."

A LITTLE figure glided through the hall;
   "Is that you, Pet?"—the words came tenderly;
A sob—suppressed to let the answer fall—
   "It isn't Pet, mamma; it's only me."

The quivering baby lips!—they had not meant
   To utter any word could plant a sting,
But to that mother-heart a strange pang went;
   She heard, and stood like a convicted thing!

One instant, and a happy little face
   Thrilled 'neath unwonted kisses rained above:
And, from that moment, "Only Me" had place
   And part with "Pet" in tender mother-love.

AWAKING A COMFORTABLE SLEEPER.

———

OME years ago there was a threatened dilapidation of my physical house. I attempted to avert the calamity, and obtained from my physician two excellent and very different prescriptions — one was a mixture of all the tonics concerning which he had any knowledge, leaving out the ingredients which Septimius Felton added, with such fatal confidence, to the marvelous drink which poor Aunt Kezia loved to decoct! The other was a trip to Europe!

Does any one feel more secure in his second voyage than he does on the first? in the twentieth than he did on the tenth? I believe not, for a friend who has crossed the ocean forty times told me that his last voyage was accomplished with an increased sense of the dangers of the sea. So I am not in the least ashamed to admit my fear of disaster on my return trip, and on board one of the stanchest ships which crosses the Atlantic.

It happened that I was obliged to share my stateroom with a stranger. As I looked over the list of passengers, I remembered that I had known many persons in America of the same name as this lady

who was booked for the upper berth in our stateroom, but as I did not know the particular family
of ——s to which she belonged, I could not guess
her probable characteristics, physical or otherwise·
How this lady discerned me on the tug which took
us from the dock at Liverpool to the ship, I never
understood; but after a few minutes she came to
me in a friendly manner, and said: " I believe we
are to spend these ten days together." I replied:
"This, then, is Miss ——. I'm glad to see you;
and (my mind was convinced by the first sight of
her true-hearted, generous countenance), I've no
doubt that we shall agree in our small apartment,
and enjoy the voyage!" We examined each other
as to our expectations in regard to sea-sickness,
and I, in an undertone, expressed the hope that she
would not be "timid," but that I might find my
courage growing stronger in the strength of her
companionship. My anxious face and inquiries
were met with joyous and inspiring smiles, and the
most assuring cheery talk. How gentle and kind
is the gracious providence of God toward me, I
thought. This dear good soul will minister sunshine and comfort to me, whether the days are
stormy or serene!

This lady was not a duplicate of every third
woman whom you may meet; she was pleasantly
and interestingly unique. There is no sign of good
nature and of honest earnestness which she lacked.
Half her breadth would almost have measured me

from shoulder to shoulder; her full blue eyes
were clear and merry, and her entire figure
had a firm, stalwart expression, which did not
in the least detract from her gentle and womanly
bearing.

"One at a time," being the rule we had adopted,
I preceded my friend the second night, and was
comfortably out of the way when she came down.
In the most orderly fashion my companion prepared
herself for rest, and with admirable agility she
climbed into her berth. I felt rather ashamed not
to offer her the lower bed, and save her this exer-
tion, but I expected to be thrown to the floor every
night by the rolling of the ship, and selfishly
dreaded the distance from the upper berth. There's
something about the sea which produces a deaden-
ing effect upon one's generosity. After expressing
hopes for each other's comfort, we began our night's
work of sleeping. I had toiled at it for about two
hours, when some extra violence of the waves
roused me to full consciousness, and set my heart
beating with the most agitating fear. I listened to
the steady, undisturbed breathing above me till I
could bear it no longer, and, raising the curtain a
trifle, I awoke that comfortable sleeper with this
miserably weak and timid question :

"Miss ——, are you awake? (I knew she
wasn't). Don't you think that the ship is going
very fast, and isn't it pitching dreadfully?"

Not vexed at all with my disturbing her slumbers,

my good friend at once replied, in a tone of assuring confidence :

"Oh, no ; why this is nothing ! You ought to have come over with us last spring ; we had a storm then that shook the ship and tossed her about like a plaything, but we rode right through it safely enough !"

"Well, don't you think the motion is *singular* to-night ; it seems to me as if" — she would not let me fill out the measure of possible terror by expressing all I felt, but she tried to cheer my spirits and enliven my views of ocean life. At last we ceased talking and I lay still, absorbed in dismal calculations as to the depth of the sea beneath the bottom planks of the ship !

By and by I heard a gentle stirring, and in tones which showed her fear of waking me, as she leaned over the edge of the berth, my companion put this question to my astonished ears :

"Did you ever chew gum ?"

"Why, yes," I replied ; "I have in my childhood chewed it ; but I don't think I want any now."

"Well, if you don't want any gum, just chew on this : '*Commit thy way unto the Lord, and He shall direct thy paths.*' Now, dear, if you are going to the bottom, the Lord knows it, and orders it ; and He will go with you !"

"Thank you," I said ; "that is a good verse to chew on ; I'll try to think of it, and sleep on it."

My friend was soon rocked to rest by the very

billows which had troubled me, and I grew more calm as I summoned my faith to control my fear. The thought of God was sweet and comforting to my heart in that lonely hour on the sea. Committing myself to my Father's will and love, I slept in peace, till the morning called us up to the sunny deck. "It is a pleasant thing for the eyes to behold the light of the sun" at sea ; and it is a blessed thing, too, to get a little sunshine from your neighbor's faith when the heavens are dark, and the waters are round about you on every side !

DID WHAT HE COULD.

HE wasn't much, anyway. He was getting old. He was plain in look, to the verge of ugliness. He had a great black blotch on one side of his face. He was illiterate; it was as much as he could well do with his stubby old pen to make out his few accounts with his custom-ers. His hands were hard with blacksmithing; and his often-bloated checks were seldom, even on Sundays, wholly free from the smut thereof. He was poor. Probably he shod many a horse which would sell almost any day at auction for more dollars than all he was himself worth. He had a bad habit of drinking intoxicants, and had been known to spend the night in the gutter. Moreover, as such men almost always are, he was profane. Little children have been known to be afraid to go by his small shop on the slope of the hill, lest they should overhear him swearing terribly, in a rage with some horse or ox which was skittish about being shod, and bothered him; it was so frightful to hear him then.

No, he wasn't much, anyway!

But he had an immortal soul under this rude and

rough outside, and he knew it. And some kind of a future stretched before him through the eternities, and he knew that. His mother — who had been sleeping more than half a century in the little mossy, bushes-over-grówn grave-yard, in sight over the fields from his front door — used to love him, and pray for him, and with her last breath consecrated him to God, and begged him to do what he could that was good, for her sake; and he knew that.

One evening the church-bell rang. It didn't often ring then. But some strange minister was paying a visit to the aged pastor, and had consented to preach for him that evening, and so the bell was rung, just at sundown. When its first notes floated off over the hills, the people, as they heard it, thought some one was suddenly dead (for they remembered no townsman known to be lying near his end), and listened to count the strokes, if they might guess whom it might be; but they soon perceived that it was ringing, and not tolling, and so they knew no one was dead, but that there was a " meeting " out of due time. So they hurried up with their evening chores, made themselves tidy, and started as quickly as they could; and by the time the bell rang its second ringing, the "teams" were coming in sight from various directions, and, one by one, tying up for the evening in the horse-sheds, as fishing vessels moor at the wharves when their day's work is done.

The blacksmith had had a good day. He had shod four horses and six oxen, and made a good thing of it. The animals had all behaved well. He himself had behaved well. He hadn't drank a drop of rum for a month — wonderful for him. He didn't remember that he had said a bad word that day — still more wonderful for him. It was partly due, and he confessed it to himself, as he thought it over, to the fact that a very sweet, pure young girl — she might be five-and-twenty — who now and then, at long intervals, rode by from the next town, had stopped that morning to get him to re-set a shoe which her horse had just cast. While he was at work, she talked to him — as " if he were somebody ; " and she had said : " Thank you *very* much, *Mister* ——," when she paid him and cantered away. This had made him feel all day more as if he were somebody than usual, and had combined with other things to make a good day for him. He was sitting on the great flat stone doorstep just outside the front door of his small cottage — where he used often to smoke his pipe of an evening, and was just filling that pipe for a smoke, when he heard the first notes of the bell. And when he had heard enough to decide that it was not a mortuary announcement, but a call to worship, he said to himself : " I haven't felt so much like a man for a year; I feel like going ; I guess I'll wash up and go. Maybe some great speaker will be there ! "

So he washed up, and got out his faithful swallow-tail, made of blue cloth with flat brass buttons, which had done duty for ever so many years, since he married his last wife, at weddings and funerals, and when he did go to meeting on Sundays — which, truth to tell, was now growing to be very seldom; and walked leisurely up to the top of the hill on whose side he lived, and down the other side, and up another to the church-yard; and after sitting on the fence, and chatting with one of his neighbors until the second bell had rung out, and he could hear them inside beginning to sing the first hymn, he got slowly down, thinking how much more spry he used to be in doing that thing years ago, and went in and took a seat in a shady place near the door.

The service went on. The good old pastor introduced his guest and friend — a young man who "talked very natural" to them for a half-hour; taking for his starting-point the text about the woman of whom Jesus comfortingly said: "She hath done what she could." He made God's commands to, and Christ's claims upon men, seem easy and just. He said *each* can do *something*. What God wants is that. "God is very fair. He doesn't ask a blacksmith to make a gold watch, but to shoe a horse, or make a nail, or forge a great iron bolt, or do something else which he can do perfectly well — if he only will." And our friend shrank further into the shadow, as he said within himself:

" That's so; and that's right. I *can* do it, and I
will." The young man — all unknowing — just as
he was closing, got round to this blacksmith again.
He said : " Now I beg you all to do God and your
Saviour this justice, *to do what you can* for them,
for yourselves and your fellow-men. Not what
you can't do, but what you can do ; surely it
is fair for God to ask that! Perhaps under some
of these silent mounds that surround us here
[waving his hand toward the church-yard] mol-
ders some tongue that once pleaded in dear dying
accents with some one of you, to live for God?
Have you done it? Have you done *what you
could?*"

The arrow went in between the joints. The
blacksmith lingered under the shadow of a horse-
shed until the retiring rattle of the last wagon was
still, and then made his way under the starlight to
the moss-grown grave whose rusty headstone bore
his mother's name. He fell upon his knees. He
knew, afterward, that he remained a long time, and
that he cried "like a child" there. He scarcely
knew how he went home. He could give, indeed,
very little rational account of his own feelings and
acts. His thoughts of God, and Christ, and of his
mother, were very much mixed up together. But
he seemed to himself to have had an interview with
all three; and to have confessed to all three the
mean wickedness of his life; and to have carried
away the feeling that all three had forgiven him —

provided he would now faithfully begin, and never, never stop doing "what he could."

The next Sunday, clean-shaven and well-washed, he astonished the congregation by three several attendances in the house of God. And in the evening prayer-meeting he amazed everybody by getting up, and — after a long pause — saying : "Good friends, I can shoe horses tolerable, and oxen some, and sich; but I aint no hand to talk. I allow I haint done what I could. And I'm awfully to blame. I want you to forgive me. I guess God has. I'm sure my good old mother has. And I'm bound to do what I can, now. I do love God. And I'm sorry I've drunk so, and swore so; and I ain't a-going to do neither no more — not if I know it. And I love everybody. And I want everybody to know that the parson here, and the deacons, and these good brethren and sisters, that have kept this meetin'us runnin' this last forty year, while I've been a-hanging on behind — and they going up an awful hard hill at that — I want everybody to know that they wuz right all along, and that I wuz just as wrong as — as 'twould be to try and weld cold iron! Now you see, as I told you, I can't talk none, but I must do suthin' to let you know that I'm a changed man. It's dreadful late in the day; but I want you to pray for me, that for the rest o' my life I may be a man *that did what he could!*"

Two months later to a day, the good parson told his wife, as he went in to her sick chamber to report his Sabbath evening service : " Molly ! that old blacksmith's speech, I almost think, has been worth more to the cause of Christ in this place than all my forty years' preaching ; surely I never knew fifty-nine persons converted, all at once so, by my sermons — and that's the number up to to-night that I count as the killed and mortally wounded from that single broadside."

" Ah ! but, husband dear, if you hadn't been preaching the forty years, his speech could not have done such execution ! Paul plants what Apollos waters."

" Yes, Molly, and God giveth increase, as pleaseth Him ! "

OUR CHRIST.

In Christ I feel the heart of God
    Throbbing from heaven through earth:
Life stirs again within the clod:
    Renewed in beauteous birth,
The soul springs up, a flower of prayer,
Breathing His breath out on the air.

In Christ I touch the hand of God,
    From His pure hight reached down,
By blessed ways before untrod,
    To lift us to our crown —
Victory that only perfect is
Through loving sacrifice, like His.

Holding His hand, my steadied feet
    May walk the air, the seas;
On life and death His smile falls sweet —
    Lights up all mysteries:
Stranger nor exile can I be
In new worlds where He leadeth me.

Not my Christ only; He is ours;
    Humanity's close bond;
Key to its vast, unopened powers,
    Dream of our dreams beyond. —
What yet we shall be, none can tell;
Now are we His, and all is well.

THE BIBLE IN THE CLOSET.

T is good to read the Bible through; but our own experience has given us an utter repugnance to all carefully constructed schemes for accomplishing that end in a given time. In the early days of our spiritual history, we met with such a plan in the memoirs of McCheyne, and immediately determined to adopt it; but we soon discovered that we had bound ourselves with the most galling chains, and we had little or no enjoyment in our Scripture study until we conclusively abandoned the course on which we had entered. It commenced, if we remember rightly, at three separate places. Genesis, Isaiah, and Matthew, and went on at the rate of so many chapters daily from each, until, at the year's end, the reader who had the patience to follow it came out at the Song of Solomon, Malachi, and Revelation. But we found that there was no principle of association between the three places selected. We discovered, also, that we had burdened our consciences with a fictitious responsibility, and felt that we had committed a grievous sin when we did not accomplish in a day "the tale" of chapters. In short, **we** were rapidly developing within us a spirit of the utmost legalism, and were beginning to feel that the great end of a religious life was the regular study of the Bible after McCheyne's plan; instead of realizing that the perusal of the word of God was only a means for helping us to live in a right, noble and manly Christian manner.

As soon as we became alive to the state of the case, we threw the whole scheme overboard, and ever since, so far as the enjoyment of the Scriptures is concerned, we have luxuriated in "the glorious liberty of the children of God." Sometimes we have taken more, and sometimes less, always "as we were able to bear it;" and the result has been, that we go to the word of God to be refreshed and strengthened, and not to perform a duty, or to fill out a plan. We eat because we are hungry, and so long as we are hungry; and therefore our enjoyment is always keen. He who takes all his food by weight and measure, and is always thinking of the right number of ounces, or the proper proportion of a quart, is apt to be a weak valetudinarian, and the attention which he gives to such little things is sure to narrow his mind and heart, so that he is inevitably a small man. Now it is quite similar in this matter of Bible-reading in the closet; and the only rule which one ought to lay down for himself is to read until his soul is satisfied. Occasionally, he will come upon a verse which will seem to him to be

like a branch heavily laden with ripe fruit, and
shaking that into his lap, he will find he has enough
for all the day. While, again, he may read a whole
book at a sitting and feel that he has not had too
much. One day a parable may be enough; another,
he will seek to have a psalm ; now he will be content with one beatitude, and again, he will read at
once the entire sermon on the mount, and see in it,
as a connected whole, a unity and completeness
which he has missed while perusing it in disjointed
chapters.

But while thus insisting that every one should
exercise his liberty in the matter of closet study of
the Scriptures, there are one or two hints which we
would give, by way of intensifying the interest
which such an occupation ought to produce.

As far as possible, each book should be read as
a whole. The chapters into which they are divided
are in many cases as artificial as the scheme to
which we have just referred. Think of a son in
Europe dividing a letter from his father in this
country into so many sections, and taking one
of these every morning for his refreshment, yet
never reading the whole epistle at once ! But it is
in this absurd fashion that many of us are content
to treat the letters of Paul and his brother apostles.
To go through the Epistle to the Romans carefully
at one sitting, is better for giving us a thorough
comprehension of its meaning and design than
many a commentary ; while with such a book as

that of Job, it will be quite impossible to attain to
any clear understanding of its purpose and argument if we take twenty-one days for its perusal at
the orthodox rate of two chapters a day.   For ourselves, we are free to confess that we never made
much of that magnificent poem, until we read it,
as one reads a book of Milton, or an idyll of Ten-
nyson; and, even after that, our ideas of its meaning were marvelously brightened when, while
teaching in a Scottish country school, we picked
out boys enough to make up the number of the
dramatis personæ, and went over it with them,
making each adhere to the pieces spoken by the
character which he represented.   It is hardly a
closet exercise, but we can conceive of nothing
more calculated to interest a family group in the
patriarch of Uz, than such a method of dealing
with the book that goes by his name.

  We add only one other hint: that we should
endeavor to get a clear idea of the circumstances
out of which the writing before us grew, and to
which it was directed.   Every scholar knows that
the books in the Old and New Testaments are not
arranged in chronological order, and can tell how
much new interest was added to his consideration
of that under his hands when he discovered its
date and primary application.   It would be well,
therefore, if in the closets of our intelligent church-
members such books as Angus's Bible Handbook
were to be found, so that they could study each

gospel, epistle, prophecy and psalm in the light of the occasion to which it belonged; while volumes like Paley's Horæ Paulinæ or Blunt's Scriptural Coincidences, or Plumtre's Biblical Studies, will help them to discover what mines of wealth there are in the by-ways of the sacred books, of which the mere surface reader takes no note. Moreover, the perusal of such works along with the Bible will suggest to us new applications of the principles on which their authors proceeded, and will make our closet hours as deeply interesting to us as their hours with the microscope and the telescope are to the entomologist and the astronomer.

3

A CONSPICUOUS CONVERSION.

IN the autumn of 1872, I met the subject of this sketch by introduction on a street corner. I had already heard something of his professional eminence in the law; and of his great natural gifts. The picture of the man, as memory now recalls him, upon that morning of first introduction, is in this perspective.

He stood straight as an arrow. His eye keen, but kindly; a lawyer's eye, trained to take in a twinkle all the telling points of another's personality. Locks, once black, were enough flecked with gray to give evidence that he was over fifty years up the hill.

Gradually I learned more of this man, whom the whole city and State knew better than we often know our next-door neighbors. In one line of legal practice he had no competitor. And in all departments of jurisprudence his stores of learning and ready use of authorities are subjects of constant remark among gentlemen of the bar. His eloquence is captivating. His cogency convincing. He can harangue a mixed crowd upon a political issue until they are hoarse with huzzas ; and then turn into the supreme court and indulge the bench with authorities quoted from memory as much as from memoranda. He is a man of iron nerve ; and has stood as undaunted in the thick of battle as if bullets were baby's playthings. His innermost pulse beats against all oppressors of the poor and lowly. He was an abolitionist when it needed almost reckless courage to declare it. He despises hypocrisy as few others do whom we have met. His nature is of that composition which makes a conquest of his heart and purse the easiest possible to the impostor.

It is a very blundering beggar who fails to make my friend's fountains of sympathy flow. He is indeed a rare and noble man — now that the gravest faults and deadliest evils have been removed by the grace of the Holy Ghost. For it must be added, that, with all his natural gifts, and endowments, and all his achievements in learning and influence, he had come to contemn the cross and all the truth it teaches. He despised religion and its professors with a bitter and derisive despite. Court practice had increased his contempt for Christians by every additional flaw that he had found in their testimony. He turned his back upon the church — except upon a sort of nondescript concern called a church, and characterized chiefly by the conspicuous absence of anything honorable to Christ.

Two years ago, subsequent to my first introduction, and to our utmost surprise, this distinguished lawyer and determined enemy of the Master, crossed the threshold of our church. Following his figure and fixing my eye on the man as he sat down, I had this impression of him. Stern, unsympathetic, seemingly disgusted before the sermon began, and growingly disgusted as it went on. I thought an angel's ear might hear his teeth whetting across each other, sharpening to cut sermon and preacher to pieces as soon as the stupid services should close. Meantime, there was to me but one man in all the crowded church. In a way all new to me, I was led to let my whole soul out in desire for his conversion. Not a farthing cared I for his cold and critical attitude. My soul went out for his soul. All the remaining duties of the day were mere variations on the theme of this man's salvation. I worked thinking of him; I slept dreaming of him. Two days of desire and prayer ended in nothing more than dropping a line into the mail, recognizing his presence the past Sabbath, and expressing my pleasure. He replied, respectfully, in a note whose edges were as keen as its touch was icy. I replied in a brief epistle, which, so far as was in me, I perfumed with love and wrapped in velvet. He responded in what seemed to me like pussy's foot, soft on the outside, claws underneath! "He was too busy to be dis. turbed." It ought not to disturb the busiest man to have a bouquet laid on his table. So I resolved to gather bouquet truths and tie them round with some texts on the atonement, and send them. Now my friend was aroused. He wanted to argue. He would show the joints of our doctrine and the deceptions of our professors. Gently but firmly I declined; confessed that he could defeat me in doctrinal difficulties; allowed the church to be below the best standards. But two things I would not do; argue, nor see him. " But," said my next note to him, "you will now and hereafter be the subject of my earnest prayer, at a certain *specified* hour of each day, until you repent or perish, or I pass away."

What unwritten events followed for a few weeks are only known in part to me; and these are too sacred to be given out. Suffice it, that the great opposer grounded every weapon; gave up every hope; made clear and comprehensive confession before God; and, accepting Christ for righteousness and redemption, presented himself as a new man. With the converted Saul's humility, he made known his previous state of sin, and his mad opposition to the truth. He had been friend, fellow and correspondent with the eminent infidels of two hemispheres. He had " cast away the entire Christian system." He believed professors to be arrant hypocrites. All this he retracted; took the humblest place. "Only let me sit down on the sill of the door; it is all I deserve," said he at his admission into the church. "Come to my house, and erect a family altar for me; and if God helps I will never permit it to be without the daily offering." It was a joyous hour when, as the pastor of that new-born family (husband and wife both starting together), I set up the altar for offering. And most faithfully has my friend fed it with daily fuel.

And now what have we? A man of more than middle life; of eminence in a profession whose members are not generally believers; a man who had led the van of those most at variance with God; a man who had at his tongue's end the keenest and completest arguments against Christianity; a man whose change would cause him the only conspicuity which a proud heart opposes; this man down as flat as Saul on the highway, and as meekly asking: "Lord, what wilt thou have me to do?" Since that day, his life has been so modestly, so definitely, so decidedly, so undeviatingly loyal, that I venture he would search in vain, who would find one to deny the mighty change in this, now, man of God.

"Ah, he was suffering some misfortune, and so was easily affected." Far from it; he was on the top of the flood-wave. "Perhaps his mental powers are failing." Is he failing who can contend in courts from morning till night; then, eating a light supper, sit down to his table and work until the breakfast bell; rise to eat, and off to court until evening, and sit down to yet a second night of

work which does not have a doze in it until daylight? Two days and two nights of steady work!
Only Frederic the Great, of those of whom I have
read, ever had such endurance.

Space is too short for detailed proof. But this
statement we boldly make. There is not another
who more bitterly disbelieved, and with better ability to give the strongest answer for his infidelity.
And to-day there is not one of whom we have
knowledge who is more meekly and lovingly sitting
at Jesus' feet, "clothed, and in his right mind."
And if any assuming and shallow scholar attempts
to show that education raises men out of the
reach of that repentance and regeneration which
humbles the head and radically changes the heart,
I shall tell him the story of this most conspicuous
of the many conspicuous cases which it has been
God's good will to give me in my ministry and pastoral care.

CONCERNING CLUB-HOUSES.

MANY people are prejudiced against clubs and club-houses. The name is enough to condemn either. Is this reasonable? Not entirely so. Every case must be judged on its own merits. Certainly, an association of a limited number of persons, who unite their moneys to provide a suitable place for personal enjoyment, often with libraries and other facilities for improvement, is not necessarily evil. Nor is it any injustice to the public, that the club restricts its privileges to members of its own body, except by inviting at its own pleasure, persons not members.

I suppose, however, that the apparent exclusiveness is a source of prejudice. Why should it be? Only a moderate number can be accommodated in any one club-house. Moreover, the members have themselves paid the cost of it. Others can institute a new club, and build a new club-house.

I have, however, lately had experience as to the exclusiveness of a club, which made it quite troublesome.

In the town where my family has been temporarily placed, **there is a club** whose superior **privi-**leges I wish to **enjoy. I can enjoy them by invita-tions from time to time, but I** greatly prefer **to do it as a right, and to meet my share of the expenses. One does** not like to be beholden, even to **friends, all the time.**

This club, unlike many, admits favored women and children to its advantages ; and my desire to get admission has been mainly for my family's sake. For a whole year have I tried in vain.

This particular club was formed some **years** ago. **It erected a** brick **building** capacious **and hand-some. It** has literary and **other** exercises **of a very** superior order, and often **has music. In fact, it is** high-toned and first **class. Its personal rights of** property **are somewhat peculiar. Instead of** owning **all in common, it had the** builder draw lines on the entire **broad lower floor ; erect** private boxes according **to** these **lines, and put** doors to the boxes, and fastenings on **the** doors. And each member of the club is an owner of a private box in fee, which also descends to his heirs. When the club-house is to be occupied, into his own box goes **the** owner, with his family and any **other** he chooses to **invite ; and** he shuts **the door and fastens it.**

In this particular **club the owner, as such, pays no part of** the expenses attending **the occu**pancy of the club-house, except **for** keeping the shingles tight, mending **any** broken **glass, and** for **an**

occasional **coat of paint.** Nothing can be required
of him even for coal or the pay of the janitor; and of
course nothing **for** the cost of any music, speakers,
and the **like.** All such expenses are met by con-
tributions of the generous. A member of the
club, that is, a proprietor; **that is, a** box-holder,
may enjoy all the advantages of **the** club-house for
all his life, and never pay one cent for its superior
privileges. He can, if he chooses, **lease** his box,
and pocket the rent.

But **a great** difficulty here **is, that** some box-
owners **who** rarely **occupy any** portion, will not
lease any **part to** those **who would occupy.** Hence
there **are** some empty boxes, while other persons
(for **instance, myself and family)** earnestly desire
the privileges.

Nor **have I,** nor has anybody **else, on** the theory
and practice of this club-house, any right to com-
plain. **The owners** paid their money honestly;
their **boxes are their own** private property, and it
is nobody's **business.** If any people do not like it,
they **can build another club-house.** Only, that is
beyond my power, or **my desire.**

Of course everybody knows that this particular
club-house is a meeting-house. I have sometimes
heard it called a House of God.

I want **to** know what to do. For more than a
year have **I tried** to get reasonable accommodation
for my family. I have tried to *hire* sittings enough.
Our number is not very large; yet have they been

divided around into three parts of the house, and some of them, even then, dependent on the courtesy of friends. Two of them had regular sittings awhile in a spot where every opening of the door sent a deluge of cold air on their necks; and only two sittings at that. Courtesy continually says to me: "Bring them into my pew any time." Yes, but, first, I want my children to sit together, and two parents, if both are there, cannot sit in three places; secondly, I want to pay for the sittings.

I take this as a sample case. What are the difficulties? Is the church crowded? No. There is a good congregation, but it would be greatly increased if sittings could be furnished. Is the house small? No. Six tiers of pews of liberal dimensions. This club-house system is here a weight around the neck of a remarkably able and successful minister. The trouble is, pews have been inherited. Owners will not part with them. Many owners decline to rent any sittings to anybody, even if they have one or five at liberty. Persons have told me how long and patiently they waited, before they could get any accommodations, while there were plenty of vacant sittings every Sunday and successive months.

You know there are four systems as to pews. (1.) Where pews are owned in fee, not subject to any taxation for current expenses. (2.) Where pews are owned by individuals, but subject to taxation for current expenses, according to a fixed original valuation. (3.) Where pews are owned by the society, and rented either annually or continuously. (4.) Where all sittings are absolutely free.

There are objections, of course, to each method. But incomparably the worst, and in the present state of society, inexcusable, is the first. We know how it originated, and that then its evils were not experienced. Now it is a barbarism. It enables an owner to enjoy all the advantages of the church, and never pay a cent therefor, as does the fourth above; but, unlike the fourth, it enables him to prevent the growth of a congregation. It makes what is called a house of God simply a club-house, whose owners have contrived to have comforts for themselves and families and invited guests; or, what a theater would be if it was all private boxes owned by individuals without taxation or rental. Anything more different can hardly be imagined — this system from one where a building is supposed to be erected, in which one is to preach the gospel to all who will listen. Not a meeting-house; a club-house. The club being, not the church, but the pew-owners.

What can one do? Go elsewhere? But here is the form of worship and the kind of doctrine my family prefer. Here is a minister, whom I esteem for his intellectual power, and love for his great, generous heart. Here is the house where I was led when I was a mere child, every inch of whose walls is familiar to me. Here are the men I knew and honored as I grew in years. And in this house, and in the seat where he had been for forty years, my dear and honored father, an officer of its church, sat only the day before God suddenly called him up higher. Can I take my children elsewhere, while his grave is under only its first snow?

ONLY TO-DAY.

ONLY to-day for sorrow!
  If God has bidden me weep,
I'll think the brightest to-morrow
  Soon over the night will creep;
And so I will only pray
That he give me grace to-day!

Only to-day for labor! —
  Each day by itself alone;
With its helping for my neighbor,
  And its watching for my own; —
And so I do with my might —
And so I walk in the light!

Only to-day for living!
  Fresh, plain to understand,
With its loving and doing and giving
  Brought close to my heart and hand, —
Since to-day, for aught I know,
Is all I shall have below!

AFTER MANY DAYS.

WAS keeping house for a friend who was suddenly called from home by the illness of a relative. One day a caller was announced, and descending to the drawing-room, an old man rose to greet me whose mantle of seventy years could not conceal a presence of rare dignity and grace. His genuine regret at my friend's absence awakened my curiosity.

"Will you leave a message for her?" I inquired.

"I think not," he replied; "only this card."

As he turned to leave the room his attention was arrested by a portrait on the wall.

"Who is this?" he eagerly asked, but immediately added, half to himself, "I see, I see — the same Clover of by-gone days."

With graceful courtesy he begged my pardon for the momentary abstraction, and said: "Will you please tell Mrs. Brayton that I hope to see her in the other house — the one not made with hands?"

This was not the language of conventional callers, and long after his departure I pondered over his half-mysterious, but strangely attractive bearing. I had been intimately acquainted with my friend from early girlhood, and it seemed impossible for her to have met this man and made such an evident impression, and I be ignorant of the circumstances. I concluded that I had entertained a very agreeable lunatic.

The next day Mrs. Brayton came home, and I gave her the stranger's card. On one side was the name and address:

ROBERT RALSTON,

Stuttgart, Germany.

beneath which was written in pencil: "I came here to answer yes to the questions of thirty years ago."

"O how sorry I am!" she exclaimed. "It is like one risen from the dead. What did he say?"

I repeated the verbal message, told her of his rapt look before the portrait, and then claimed an explanation of such strange proceedings. My curiosity was rewarded with the following story:

"Years ago," said my friend, "when a mere child of seven, I was sent away from home to escape a contagious disease which had broken out among the children in our town. I was shut up in a lonely house with a maiden lady, a friend of mother's, and I well remember the terrible homesickness of the first few days. Separated from a large circle of brothers and sisters, and from the free, loving ways of our household, the gloom and grandeur of this other place nearly crushed me. Only a lack of courage kept me from running away. One day this lady's brother came home. He was a bronzed, bearded man of forty, who had spent years in traveling, and he delighted my hungry heart with wonderful stories of what he had seen in other lands. Day after day he gave himself up to the task of amusing me. Never did lady have a more devoted knight. It was the winter season, and every pleasant day he coasted down hill with me, or took me out for brisk walks in the quiet town, teaching me to observe and enjoy a thousand things which my childish eyes would not have seen but for his kindly instructions. He taught me to sing, and led me into the most enchanting realms in the world of books, training my mind, even then, to discriminate between the true and false. We played checkers a great deal, and so delicate was the tact which allowed me to beat that I never dreamed it was not the result of my own skill.

"I had a little trick of humming to myself as I poised my finger over the men, deliberating a move. One day he exclaimed with an air of having made a rare discovery: 'Why, it must be the humming which makes you so successful! I think I'll try it.' Then he, too, would hum so musically that I would wait the game to listen, but it seemed to avail him nothing. Then he would declare that there must be some witchery in my tones.

" 'Why do you call me Clover?' I once asked him. 'My name is Alice.'

" 'Because clover blossoms are bright and bonnie, and so are you,' was the reply.

" I cannot understand, even now, how this cultured man of the world was content to give himself up so fully to the task of pleasing a little child. I was sorry when the summons came to return home, and the night before my departure I was permitted to sit up beyond the usual time. I can recall just how the room looked. The candles were not lighted, and the glow from the blazing logs on the hearth made fantastic shadows on the wall. The furniture was of massive oak, curiously carved, and in that weird light each article seemed to take the form of a horrible monster, that made me nestle in the strong arms of my friend with a delightful sense of safety. Although I could not understand much of the conversation, I felt that he and his sister were talking wisely and well of men and affairs. Finally they drifted on to the subject of religion, and something in the man's cold belief — or unbelief — chilled my young heart. The life of Jesus Christ was analyzed in the same critical way as that of Lord Burleigh and Napoleon Bonaparte.

" Suddenly I lifted my head from his shoulder and asked, with astonishment, 'Don't you love Jesus, Mr. Ralston?' The only reply was a hand gently forcing my head back to its resting-place,

4

and the conversation continued with his sister. I could endure it no longer and again lifted my head to inquire, with childish persistence, 'Well, don't you believe Jesus loves you?' This time not only was a hand laid tenderly upon my curls, but something like a tear dropped on my upturned face, as he said softly, 'I believe in *you*, Clover, with all my heart.' The next morning he kissed me good-bye as he put me in the old stage-coach, and from that day to this I have never heard of him."

The bit of pasteboard in my friend's fingers grew-luminous with a life's imagined history. Time had brought her the ordinary experiences of girl, and wife, and motherhood, but who could guess where and how his days had been spent? In what lands had he wandered, seeking but finding no rest for the uneasy soul, until he found it in Him who is the Peace of a weary world.

"A little child shall lead them," even after many days.

A TALK WITH MINISTERS.

HERE are only seven days, of twenty-four hours each, in every week; during which a working pastor must prepare two sermons, conduct from one to three prayer-meetings, make such pastoral calls and discharge such duties as the requirements of the parish may demand. To say nothing of needless invasions on his time by people who have no claim on him, and the hours consumed by attention to correspondence more or less extended, how can the average pastor find time for such courses of study as to fit him for growing usefulness? That the problem is not insoluble is plain from the fact that scores and hundreds of men have been able, for many successive years, to meet the demands of their parishes to growing acceptance, with energy sufficient to write for the papers, contribute to the magazines and quarterlies, and join the fraternity of authors. And inquiry proves that all this has been done, not by the aid of miracle, but by a wise husbanding of time and force, and by downright hard work.

It may be said, in a general way, that in such matters every man must be a law unto himself.

Men differ widely in their native capacity for
intense and continuous work, in their powers of
endurance, in rapidity of mental activity, in retent-
iveness of memory, in literary tastes, in their disposition to confine themselves to definite methods.
Samuel Hopkins speaks of studying fourteen
hours each day. Calvin found time to preach every
day, lecture three times a week, conduct a vast
correspondence, and prepare for the press his volu-
minous commentaries. Such examples are profitable for inspiration, but hardly for imitation. The
average working pastor will be fortunate if he can
succeed in following the illustrious Thomas Chal-
mers, and devote, on an average, five hours each
day to his studies. In the most active years of his
ministry he may not be able to command even such
an amount of time for uninterrupted and close
study. But there must be something seriously at
fault, if he fail, during the first ten years of his
professional life, to spend at least five hours a day
in his library. During these years he has most
leisure. The calls for outside labor are compara-
tively few. And if these years have been diligently
improved, the capacity for work will have doubled
and trebled, so that one hour may be made to do
the work of three. Dr. Alexander is right in saying that the first ten years of any minister's work
are the period in which he makes his greatest
attainments. These are years of foundation building. They determine his practical aims, his literary

or theological tastes, his methods. And where these ten golden years have been allowed to run to waste, or have been indifferently improved, it may be seriously doubted whether the loss can ever be made good.

There must be also, from the very beginning, a very definite purpose of solid improvement, a determination conscientiously made and firmly adhered to, not to sacrifice the student to the preacher. Every pastor very soon is confronted by the question : " How much time ought I to give to pulpit preparation, and how much to general study ?" These two lines of work cannot be separated; they are like the right and left lobes of the lungs ; an injury to one is hurtful to the other. He who neglects general study will soon exhaust his material, and fail in the power of public religious teaching. It would seem to be fair to divide the six days of the week equally between these two great classes of work. One half of each working day might be given to the sermon, and the other half to study ; or the first three days might be devoted to study, and the work of pulpit preparation might be begun on Thursday. In some respects, the latter plan has its peculiar advantages. It supplies time for creating mental momentum, a quality invaluable for broad and effective work. Nor will the sermon necessarily suffer. He who cultivates what has been called the " homiletical mood " will frequently find the richest and most practical themes in the course of his most general studies. Besides, where the afternoons are devoted, as they always should be, to parish work, the mind will often so combine the studies of the morning with the living wants of men, as to provoke the most profitable trains of reflection. It may be said that he finds the most numerous and the freshest themes for the pulpit, who most eagerly and gladly loses himself in surveying the broad fields of divine truth. It will be found, too, that where such a policy is early adopted, the time for general study may be gradually extended, without detriment, to careful preparation for the services of preaching. As material accumulates, as the knowledge of the Bible, and of doctrinal history, becomes more accurate and extended, as the mental powers become more vigorous, and practical sympathy with men gathers fiber and force, an hour or two may suffice for what once required an entire morning; and so, as duties and calls multiply, the acquired ease may still leave a generous margin for general study.

Equally important is it that the lines of study be carefully chosen, and firmly adhered to. A minister ought to be a man of liberal culture. But he is not summoned to be an expert in every department of human knowledge. In science, in polite literature, in political economy, in philosophy, even, he need not blush to confess his inferiority to many a man in the press; but in Christian theology and

ethics he ought to be a leader of his people, in
reality as well as in name. As a preacher of righteousness he ought to understand his subject, both
in its ideal and practical aspects. So that it would
seem only reasonable that a working pastor's time
for study should be mainly given to such departments as are immediately related to ethics and
theology. If his means are limited, he should all
the more jealously economize his dimes and dollars,
that he may possess himself as rapidly as possible
of such books as represent the very best Christian thinking in interpretation, systematic theology,
church history and the history of doctrines. .

Only too many libraries of ministers give evidence that they have been collected without any
definite plan; and many a man who displays a
couple of hundred of indifferently good books,
with the complaint that he cannot afford the luxury
of a working library, might have possessed himself,‐
without a dollar's additional expense, of a small,
but permanently valuable, collection of first-class
books. It requires some courage not to buy a new
book, fresh from the press, and loudly heralded;
but it is generally safe for a working pastor to wait
until criticism has been passed on the venture by
some competent authority. Many a dollar may be
saved by having the study-table regularly visited by
some standard Review, whose book notices are
scholarly and reliable. In the meantime it is best
to master that which is positive and reasonably

well established. It is infinitely better to be master
of the history of truth, than to be familiar with all
the shades of error. Some ministers study here-
sies too much, and truth too little; and the consequence is not only injurious to their hearers, but
also to themselves. The firmness of their intellectual fiber gradually relaxes, until positiveness of
personal conviction almost disappears.

There should also be mental vigilance, as related
to such subjects as from time to time are thrust
into public prominence. Not long since the nature
and duration of future punishment excited particular attention. More recently the Prophetic Conference gave a temporary publicity to pre-millenial
views. A wide-awake pastor will be likely, for a
time, to abandon his particular line of study, and
enter upon a more thorough exegetical, historical,
and theological mastery of the questions in debate.
It argues ill for a minister, if at such times he can
be satisfied with what he reads in newspapers and
pamphlets and magazines; especially if the question in hand has never been thoroughly considered
by him. And even where the ground has been
traversed there will be great profit in passing over
it again, under the stimulus of a wide-spread popular interest.

After all, every man must hew his own way
through the forest. He cannot walk in another's
track. He must plunge boldly into the mazes
before him, undiscouraged by early failures and

repeated crossings of his path, determined to force
his way through to where compass and chart direct
him.   Many, if not most men, have never found
time to think out a definite method; and where
such a method has been adopted, it has been of
short duration.   They simply do the work; they
have had a general and fixed aim, and have
advanced towards it, sometimes painfully, slowly
and laboriously, sometimes easily, rapidly, and with
great delight; always under the sense of imperfec-
tion and incompetence.   This question of ministerial work recurs to every pastor in some form;
and none ask it more eagerly and earnestly than
they who seem in their lives to have answered it.
Let every man do what he can; and let Christ be
the Master under whose eye we study and preach.

CASUISTRY OF THE CONFESSIONAL.

THE mistress and the Irish cook are in colloquy.

"Indade, missus, and what for should I stale from ye? I must go and tell it all to the priest. I kneel down to confess me sins; and he asks me so many questions; there's nothing in me that he doesn't find out. I daren't tell *him* a lie. I must tell him just what I took from ye, and all about it: the tay, the sugar, the coffee, and all unbeknownst to ye. He asks me jist what it was all worth, and I must tell him to a penny; for I mustn't tell a lie to *him*, ye know. 'Is that all?' he says, says he. 'Ye stop and think, and tell me ivery thing;' and his eyes look into me very sowl, and I takes care to put it high enough to be sure of me sowl. Then he says to me, says he: 'Have ye got the money wid ye?' I says, 'Yes, Father B.' Ye know ye must have the money about ye whin ye go to confess. And thin he points up to the poor-box, hanging there before me eyes; and he says, says he: 'See that ye don't lave this house till ye've put ivry penny of that ye stole into the

box yonder, fornent the post.' And I must do it,
missus, jist as he tells me, wid his eyes looking at
me so; or I go home wid a lie to the priest; and
thin what's the good of confessing, and what
becomes of me sowl? So what's the good to me,
if I stales your sugar?"

The above was a veritable occurrence in the city
of Boston, not long ago. It carries internal evidence of truth, so far as this — that an Irish servant
would not be likely to *originate* the adroit casuistry
of giving to the poor the proceeds of her pilfering.
Some shrewder mind than hers started that idea.
But is that the casuistry of the confessional? A
certain old book declares of the Almighty: "I hate
robbery for burnt offering."

A REMARKABLE CONVERSION.

ALL sudden conversions have in them something phenomenal, something antagonistic to the usual habits of thought or action of the person converted. Yet upon minute examination, a slender thread, perhaps almost invisible, connects the change of heart with some faint impression made before. It may have been words heard in childhood, imperfectly understood then, and forgotten as soon as heard, a sermon, a prayer, an admonition, a chance text of Scripture, utterly disregarded at the time, but which by some subtle power springs into active life and clamors at the closed gates of the soul. Whatever we may have heard or seen through life, may return to us without calling it a miracle. Remorse for great, sins works its own special conversions also. The recoil of the human soul from crime propels it in the opposite direction, where forgiveness for that crime can alone be sought and found. Strange and unexpected as these conversions may be where a man is born suddenly into a new life, as I before remarked, a slender link usually binds it to the past.

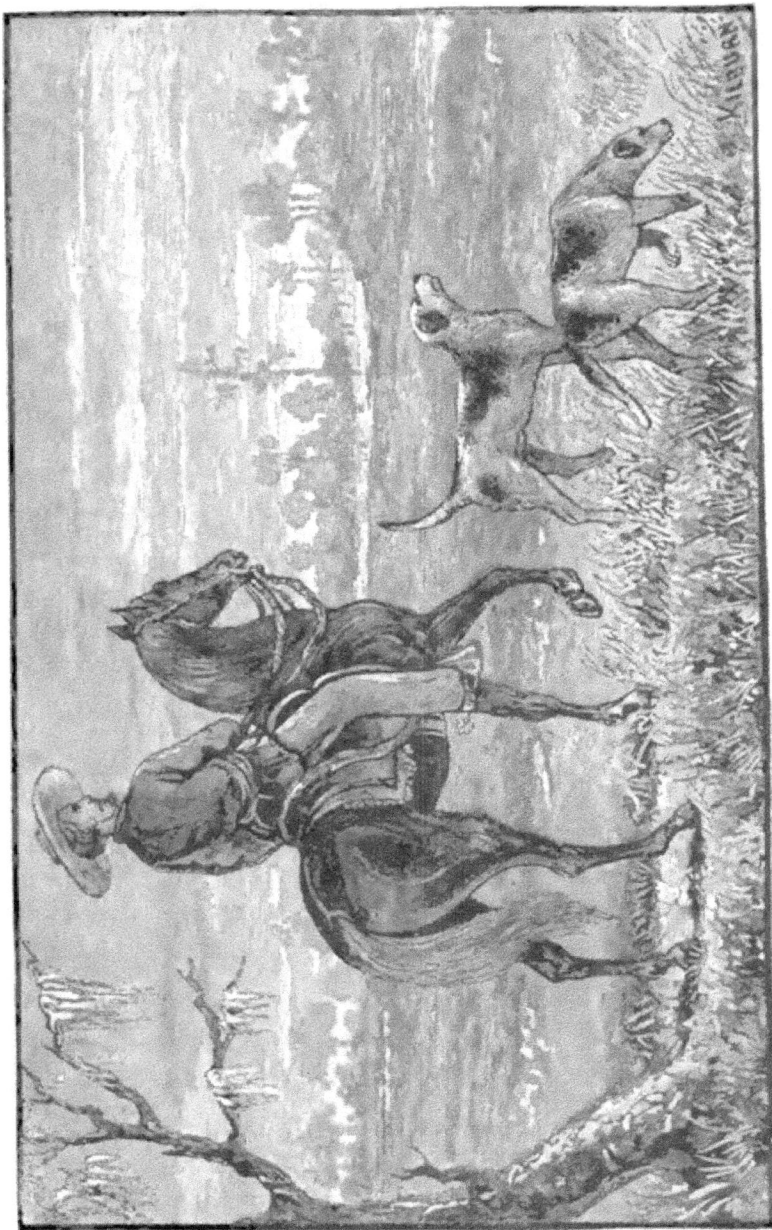

" He started on horseback one Sunday for the hog range."   Page 61.

But the instance I am about to relate is utterly devoid of all these explicable circumstances. In the parish of St. Landry, in Louisiana, the Stagg family have lived for several generations. They are French creoles, and Roman Catholics, though from the name their ancestors were probably Germans, and perhaps Protestants. The family are noted in this community for moral lives, and strict integrity in all their dealings with their neighbors.

Adolph Stagg, about thirty years of age, like the rest of his family, was very industrious, a good husband, father, and neighbor; a quiet, deliberate man, perfectly satisfied with himself, his work, his manner of life, and without a thought that anything more was needed. He had no more religious convictions than the stones in his path, and felt no more need of them. As a boy he had probably gone to mass sometimes, but like most Catholic creole men, he seldom or never entered a church. As for Protestantism, he knew nothing about it but the name, and had never read a page in the Bible in his life.

Some years ago, he started on horseback one Sunday for his hog range, intending to kill some for himself and a neighbor. Like the rest of his creole neighbors, Sunday was his usual day for attending to his stock, and doing any work outside of the crop — in fact it was with him always the busiest day in the week. The idea of anything wrong connected with this desecration of the

Sabbath never entered his mind. He had done it from a boy; his father before him, and the community in which he lived, had made it an habitual thing. He had never read, heard, or seen anything to impugn its perfect propriety. He stopped for a neighbor to assist in the hunt, and they rode together to the range.

The first singular and inexplicable circumstance to Mr. Stagg, in this day of marvels, was that not a single hog could be found, though he knew the range was full of them. His dogs were well trained, and the difficulty usually lay in selecting from large droves; but this day the dogs did not once follow the trail, and all the stock had vanished utterly. Until noon he hunted, growing more and more perplexed, when a rain coming up, he and his companion turned their faces homeward. He is a taciturn man, and with his mind full of the disappearance of his stock and the possible causes of it, he rode on in silence. He says: "Suddenly, as if by a lightning's flash, all thoughts were swept away, and a terrible pressure, almost physical in its pain, seemed to crush down my very soul. Somehow I, who had never thought of sin before, realized that it was weighing me down, and that it would destroy me if I could find no relief."

Like Saul on his journey to Damascus, smitten through and through, quivering in every nerve, his soul cried out: "Lord, what wilt thou have me to do?" for he became conscious that the Lord was dealing with him. He does not know how long the struggle lasted, probably not more than an hour or so, but before Mr. Stagg dismounted at his own door, the work was done, and the dark, ignorant soul, irradiated by divine light, understood where and how to seek salvation. There was no thought of going to a Catholic priest for help. Mr. Stagg says the flash which showed him the necessity of regeneration also seemed to point to the Bible alone as his succor. He had made only one remark to his companion during their silent ride: "You've seen me always hunting on Sunday; you will never see it again."

Like a man in a dream, he went into his house and hunted up a Bible, which strangely enough happened to be there. In Roman Catholic households the Bible is the last book you may expect to find. He knew nothing of the contents of the volume, or what he was to find in it, nor where to look for the pages which would bring him aid. He only knew that the Book would enlighten him, and he gave himself up to the guidance which had led him into this strange path. He called his wife, and together they read and studied; he eagerly, hungrily, like a starving man clutching for the bread which is to sustain life. In that first reading he found it.

After a few weeks of study and prayer, he and his wife connected themselves with the church.

Some years afterwards he entered the ministry, and has preached ever since with power and suc·cess.

You will doubtless ask why this humble individual, without special gifts of mind or fortune, should have been thus favored by this manifestation of God's grace. In many cases God's purposes remain shrouded in mystery, but in this one the answer is clear enough for all men to understand. The French creole race in the country parishes of Louisiana, particularly those of Acadian descent, is a peculiar one. There is no general culture, and a kind of light-hearted avoidance of all grave topics. The women are all superstitious and bigoted Roman Catholics. The men have a kind of hereditary belief that there is only one true church, and that the Catholic; but they are rarely seen at its services, and they only call in its aid three times in their lives, to be christened, married, and receive extreme unction on a death-bed. That they consider sufficient to wash away all sins, and ensure an easy place in purgatory. It is the business of those they leave behind them by prayers and masses to relieve them from that very unpleasant region; so they do not concern themselves much about it.

The most eloquent and gifted American clergyman could never reach these people. Both ignorance and prejudice would arm them against him. But when one of themselves, brought up amongst them, and under the same influences, living their lives, thinking their thoughts, speaking their language, comes before them with an evangel mysteriously learned, they listen and are taught. The circumstance, too, that instead of being like themselves of a mercurial, impulsive temperament, this new teacher has always been grave and unexcitable, gives his words added force. His calm, deliberate judgment and punctilious truthfulness had always made him an authority among his people, and they can never suspect him of spiritual delusion. They see him, once so calm, now full of a fervid zeal for their conversion and enlightenment, and they are awed and impressed. He has made many converts and is now in the full tide of successful labor. He is sowing the seed for a great harvest he may not live to gather ; but there will always be reapers in the field. An humble, zealous Christian, he finds his joy in doing the work of the Master who has called him to it, and leaving the fruits for other laborers in the Lord's vineyard.

5

WATCH AND CARE.

H E was a young man, who had abandoned his interest in religion. He had become used to neglecting all its observances, had resumed many former habits of recklessness, and was going rapidly in the wrong direction, a great stumbling-block to some who were querying as to the reality of Christianity. She was his neighbor, a member of the same church, a very busy woman, with a family to be cared for, and not acquainted intimately with him. She saw how he was living, and she was troubled.

She felt that her pledge to watch over her fellow church-members in love, was full of solemn meaning and included him. She believed, as she had reason to believe, in prayer. She began to pray for him. She was in earnest, too. It cut her to the heart that a professed Christian should be dis-loyal. She was as truly distressed at the peril of his soul as though he had been her own son; more than she ever had been at bodily danger, and she had faced death more than once. She believed, also, that God loved and longed for that straying soul more than she could. She prayed mightily.

She prayed often, at times incessantly. While she. worked she was pleading with God for the wanderer.

One day she met him accidentally. Tremblingly she mustered courage to ask him to return to his Saviour, and to tell him that she was interceding for him. He did not repel her, nor did he give the least evidence of heeding her words. Weeks passed. She prayed on and on, convinced, as if it depended upon her earnestness alone, that the salvation of a soul was at stake. And after weary months of patient pleading with God her reward came. She saw the young man in his seat at church. Then he appeared again in the prayer-meeting. At last she saw him at the Lord's table once more, humble, penitent, earnestly longing, if perchance so great a sinner might be forgiven, to begin again as one of Christ's own. He told her afterwards that the knowledge of her prayers in his behalf was the influence which, under God, had saved him.

In every neighborhood there are just such erring professors of religion. In every case such prayers as hers will be honored and answered of God. Do you know any such needy soul? Is there none whom you have covenanted to watch over as a fellow disciple? Are you praying thus for that soul? If not, why not?

THE FEAST OF THE ESCALADE.

N the twelfth of December, no true Geneva family fails to have its turkey on the spit; and even those dispersed in the ends of the earth hold festival, and tell each other of the traditions of the brave days of old, and especially of the heroic story of the Escalade. This story, as it has been told every year now (in 1876) for two hundred and seventy-two years, runs on this wise:

For nearly seventy years the little heretic city of Geneva had sat within its walls on its hill-top at the outlet of Lake Leman, in the enjoyment of its liberty and its religion. Violence, stratagem, treachery, all had been resorted to in vain by its old tyrants, the dukes of Savoy, to recover the foothold they once had within it. All the craft and power of the Papacy had been applied to break down this rampart of liberty for all Europe, to extinguish this radiant focus of light for all the world. It had become the asylum of the exiled martyrs of Italy and France. Said a Pope to the Duke of Alva, just starting for his ferocious campaign in the Low Countries: "Can't you go a hundred miles out of your way and stamp out that nest of heretics at Geneva?" The documents of the time teem with indications of the malignity of feeling toward Geneva throughout Catholic Christendom. At last, however, the designs against the town seemed to be given up. Pressed by military reverses, the duke had signed a treaty with Henry IV of France, at Vervins, in 1598, by which the peace of Geneva was guaranteed. And the harrassed and war-worn town had rest for a time.

Rumors of plots for its destruction kept coming from various quarters to the ears of the watchful magistracy, and a "gunpowder treason" within its walls was detected and foiled; but the natural anxiety resulting from these things was assiduously soothed by fair and friendly words from the duke and his officers.

But in November, 1602, a letter was received by the magistrates from a secret friend at Turin, describing certain portentous preparations which he himself had witnessed, and the destination of which was freely hinted. "I have witnessed experiments," he wrote, "with terrible engines of war destined against Geneva. There are hurdles for crossing a moat, and scaling-ladders on a new plan, trimmed with black cloth, and with grappling irons at the end; they shut up with a slide into small compass, and can be lengthened out without noise, so as in a twinkling to reach to the hight of your ramparts. The duke seems delighted with the preparations, and says that he has men in Geneva who will set fire in different places at the moment of the attack. Be on your guard day and night."

The alarm of the Genevese was soothed by renewed and solemn protestations of friendship on the part of Savoy, and the plot went on ripening in the dark. The general direction of it was in the hands of a renegade Frenchman, D'Albigny, Lieutenant-General of Savoy, and the execution of it was committed to Bernolière, commandant at Bonne. The troops began to assemble quietly at different points of rendezvous. At La Roche were 1,000 Spaniards, trained in the arts of massacre in American campaigns ; there were 400 Neapolitans with 500 horsemen at Bonneville; these were the contribution of the king of Spain. Four thousand of the "bloody Piedmontese," under the command of 100 Savoyard nobles, took post in the neighborhood. And at Bonne Bernolière drew out his picked force of 800 Savoyards, and explained to them the nature of the enterprise. "All I ask," he said, " is one hour of courage and fidelity." As he moved with his troops down the valley of the Arve, one company after another fell punctually into the line of march. It was night already when they rounded the shoulder of the little Salève, and the lights of Geneva, a two-hours' march distant, twinkled through the darkness. At this point a figure muffled and disguised, emerged from a cottage, attended by a retinue, and received the humble salutations of the commanding officers.

The courage of the troops rose to a high pitch when the fact was whispered that it was Duke Charles Emmanuel, who had crossed the Alps to witness the victory that was to give him the title of king, and open to him a magnificent career of conquest and empire, ending in the extinction of the Protestant powers of Europe.

The whole force, several thousand strong, moved down the course of the Arve, screened by the thickets on its banks, towards the devoted city. For a password they were to imitate the croaking of the frogs. At midnight they were posted within earshot of the city wall, and Bernolière, with his forlorn hope of 300 men in complete armor, bearing the apparatus that had been elaborated in the armories of Turin, crept up to the town, descended into the moat, and stood with bated breath against the rampart. All was still in the town. Noiselessly the muffled scaling-ladders slid in their grooves and stretched themselves up to the hight of the parapet. A Scotch Jesuit, Alexander Young, moved from man to man, whispering words of encouragement, and distributing amulets that were to keep the wearer safe from sword, water and fire. This done, the three hundred went swiftly up the wall, and stowed themselves behind the parapet. A solitary watchman, drowsing in a neighboring sentry-box, was throttled and murdered before he could utter a cry. The first and most perilous step was successful.

Bernolière despatches a messenger to D'Albigny, at the head of the reserve, and he, elated with the news, sends couriers at once to the monarch waiting anxiously on the brow of the Saleve. Success seems sure; and without further waiting, the couriers of Charles Emmanuel ride forth towards Turin, Rome, Paris and Madrid, announcing that " the Protestant Babylon " is fallen.

Much, however, remains to be done. As in most old towns, there was to be traced within the rampart the line of an earlier wall, marked by unbroken blocks of building, with here and there a gateway, now unfortified, and only negligently guarded. The whole matter had been completely studied. There were to be five companies, each under the command of an officer familiar with the place. One was to rush down to the river gate by the Rhone bridge; one was to burst a passage through the block of houses next them, and so get into the principal street; a third should attempt the little gate and steep, narrow, crooked street of the Tertasse; a fourth should climb the Treille, and enter by the great gate near the City Hall and Arsenal; and the fifth party, equipped with axes and petards, were to hasten to the inside of the great gate of the outer fortifications, surprise and overpower the guard, and, planting the petard, were to blow open the gate, sally forth and let down the drawbridge, and give free ingress to D'Albigny and his army, who waited for the explosion as their signal to approach.

But Bernolière has resolved to await the first gleam of dawn before beginning this complex operation. Meanwhile the men in armor are lying hid behind the parapet. But about two o'clock, a light is seen approaching along the rampart. It is a patrol making its round. With desperate and instant resolution the invaders spring from their ambush upon the watchmen, and pitch five of them down into the moat ; but in the struggle a gun goes off, and one of the number, the drummer, escapes, running for his life toward the river-gate, drumming furiously as he goes. All is discovered. The attack is ordered instantly. But the big bell of St. Peter's begins to boom out its alarm, and the startled citizens, half-dressed and half-armed, swarm into the dark streets to defend their homes. The first fight was at the river-gate. The Spaniards had forced the first barrier, and came screaming through the vaulted passage with shouts of triumph and cries of " Kill ! kill ! " but were met by the crowd of citizens, and driven back. Elsewhere in the streets the fight was fierce and bloody. But for all their armor, the Spaniards were forced backwards toward their place of entrance, leaving their dead behind them. The hope of success now lay in the admission of the reserves. The petard party soon overcame and dispersed the guard posted within the gate, but not till one of these had let fall the portcullis, interposing thus a fatal delay between the petardier and his work. One of the escaped guard hurried to a neighboring bastion and touched off a cannon loaded to the muzzle with nails and old iron, and trained along the line of the rampart. Down came the scaling-ladders, broken and shattered ; and the retreating invaders, arriving at the parapet, had no choice but to make the leap, with all their crushing weight of armor on, or to give themselves up as prisoners, to be hung as burglars and assassins. The sound of the cannon was understood by D'Albigny as his signal to advance, and he hurried to the gate to discover that the enterprise was a failure. There is no course left him but the back track. On his way, he meets Charles Emmanuel with his retinue, coming down with martial music to make his triumphal entry into Geneva. "Turn back, my lord! all's lost," was the general's salutation. "You wretched blockhead ! a pretty mess you have made of it," was the royal reply. And without further words the monarch took his way toward Turin. The first good news had gone before him, and every village through which he had to pass was decorated to greet the conquerer. But the strangest encounter of that humiliating march was when the duke came, at Annecy, upon a train of mules laden with church furniture and decorations, to be used when Francis de Sales, who was deeper in this scoundrelly plot than his biographers admit, should say his Christmas mass in the Geneva Cathedral.

When at last the tardy morning dawned, after

" Down came the scaling ladders, broken and shattered."   Page 74.

the longest night in all the year (the morning of
December 12th, the 22d, new style — just eighteen
years before the landing at Plymouth), and the
crowds stood gazing at the pools of blood, the
broken ladders, the battered armor, and the corpses
of friend and foe strewing the street, some one
bethought him to go to the house where old Theo-
dore de Beza, last survivor of the Reformers, infirm
and very deaf, had slept the night through unconscious of the storm that had been roaring all about
him. They led the old man to the scene of the
fight, and when he had been made to understand
the strange story, he pointed up to the great church
and said: "Come, let us go up to the house of the
Lord." And there, standing in the pulpit, he gave
out, in Beza's version, the 124th Psalm: "If it had
not been the Lord was on our side;" and that is
the Psalm which, every year, as the anniversary
comes round, they sing in memory of the great
deliverance.

When you come to Geneva, go to the Arsenal,
and look at the ingenious scaling-ladders, the dark
lanterns, the petard, still loaded, that was to have
blown up the gate, and at the suits of Spanish
armor, still holding arquebus and halberd in their
gloves of steel, and gazing grimly through their
visors at the relics of their atrocious and unsuc-
cessful crime, and call to mind the story of The
Escalade.

THE UNHARMED ROCK.

My home in boyhood was beside the sea;
And evermore, far as the eye could sweep,
Old Ocean lay outstretched. . . . . .
There was a grand old Rock that, from the main
Off a few furlongs, lifted its huge form
Up from the deep, o'erspreading many a rood,
And rearing high in air its craggy head.
All gray with time, and scarred with fissures rude,
It seemed, where stood its ponderous masses piled,
Compact together, as if giant hands,
At some forgotten date, had heaped them there
To stand amidst the sea a monument
Of giant might, in mockery of weak man;
Or as some wandering star, its orbit lost,
Had into earth been hurled, and plunging down
Sheer through the startled waters, had itself
Fast planted in its bed to move no more.

O hoary Rock! 'tis many and many a year
Since, in my boyhood's sports, I climbed thy sides,
Hid in thy clefts, or from some angle cast
The tempting bait, or on thy summit stood
Well pleased and yet half-awed, beneath my feet
To feel thee motionless 'mid tumbling floods.
E'en then came deeper thoughts, that stirred by thee
Chastened my lighter moods; thoughts of the years,
The ages, through which thou hadst changeless lain,

Thy rough stern features to the sky upturned ;
Thy cliffs unyielding, which ten thousand times
Huge billows had assailed that thundering came
With mighty onset and o'erwhelming seemed.

.   .   .   .

The memory of thee, grand Rock, instructs
My riper thought.   For me to-day thou stand'st
Of Truth the symbol ; — Truth by God unveiled
In majesty divine ; — the Word from heaven ; —
The Truth itself, whose name is CHRIST ; — a name
Sounded through ages by prophetic lyres ;
Foundation sure of man's immortal hope.
Builded on this, Church of the living God,
Securely hast thou through the centuries stood,
And standest still, amid time's surging seas,
And shalt, till time itself shall be no more !

Dark Unbelief, dim wisdom born of earth,
Still, if thou wilt, thy venturous charge renew !
A thousand times repulsed, go yet again
And try the bootless onset.   Learn once more,
To thine own shame, how impotent thou art,
When from God's Truth, unharmed, thy blows recoil,
And shivered at thy feet thy weapons lie ;
As backward from the surge-repelling Rock —
Itself unmoved — are flung the headlong waves !

HOW TO READ HISTORY.

HE idea often entertained in regard to read-ing history would be amusing if it were not pitiable.   People say, as if announcing inevitable trial : " I really must read some history ; I am mortified that I have read so little.   Would you begin with Rollin ? "

" Why Rollin ? "

" I supposed one had to begin with him."

The tone becoming still more tragical.   Then I arouse myself.

" Do you really want to read history ? "

" Yes," — sadly but firmly.

" Why ? "

" Because everybody ought to know something of the past."

" Why ? " I persist.

" Well, look at yourself, for instance ; your knowl-edge of history adds so much to your pleasure when you travel, and seems to help you so much in your criticisms of the life and literature of to-day."

" But why do you sigh as if you were a martyr ? "

" Because I hate history ; it is dull, it is con-fused ; I cannot remember it."

" Do you forget the novels you read last summer, or the people you met at the seashore?"

" Certainly not; but they are different. Why, the novels were interesting, and the people were either so charming or so disagreeable, so brilliant or so stupid, that I must be a dunce to forget them."

" Is there no one among all historical people that you care about?"

" Yes; I should like to know about Richard the Lion Hearted."

" Then, in the name of all that is sensible, why, if you want to find out about Richard of the Lion Heart, do you begin with Rollin's Ancient History?"

" I supposed you had to take a course."

And again appears the tone of heroic melancholy, as if " taking a course" was only a little less to be deplored than scaling the enemy's works with the forlorn hope. Now what should I do if I was oppressed with a sense of responsibility towards history, and the only person I cared about within her ranks was he of the Lion Heart? Go to Lingard's endless volumes; to Hallam's Middle Ages; Milman's Latin Christianity, or any of the ponderous histories of the Crusades? No, I should put my magic lantern in order, hang up my screen and throw upon it again and again those marvelous pictures of my hero from Ivanhoe, The Talisman and the Betrothed. Through these pictures I should sit beside Richard in palace and chamber; should kneel with him at the high altar, and strike with him on the tented field. I should look into his bright blue eyes; should see his yellow hair waving in the soft southern air; and dare say for a time should not care where or in what century he lived his mortal life.

But after I knew Richard as I know my own brothers, I should surely ask, who is the lovely woman he alternately caresses and despises? His Queen Berengaria? How came she his Queen? Why lingers she here on these blood-stained sands instead of living at ease in the stately palaces of distant England? Ah, you see I am driven to Agnes Strickland's Lives of the Queens of England, without dreaming of them as history at all. Fancy how I should devour every word of her record! Those with whom she spent her days, whom she loved, whom hated, would be to me more than the companions of my own bed and board. And as I note how after some act of weakness or folly she crouches terror-stricken before her enraged husband, and read that with all the violence of his race he roughly thrust her from him, shall I not inquire, what was this man's race that he excuses his savage excesses by saying: "As of old the Plantagenet is the offspring of a fiend?" And the brothers with whom he was always striving, and that Philip, who sent like wildfire through Europe the warning cry: "Look out for yourselves, the devil is loose again," when he escaped from one of his innumerable captivities, can I rest until I know all that any one knows of them ?

And as I find myself in the presence of his parents, that Henry and that Eleanor of bitter memory, and see the latter hunting, like a sleuth hound, the husband for whom she had sinned so grievously to the hidden bower of Rosamond, and ever after, in burning revenge, stirring up the fiery hearts of their wretched brood of sons against him ; or hear the shrill cries of Becket's murderers disturbing the midnight dreams of shuddering Europe, and, last of all, shrink with horror from the blasphemous curse that Henry flings back upon his God as he writhes on his frenzied death-bed, must I not find out what age of this unhappy world could harbor so much of human misery ? And as Plantagenet, Angevin Norman and Saxon, cross and recross the confused pages, shall I not be driven to Freeman's Norman Conquest lest my brain should reel in its frenzy of ignorance ?

No fear of any stopping now. I shall trace the stream to its source, and even reach Rollin in time. I shall not be contented with rapid strides in that direction alone. I shall insist on understanding each particular in the lives of those who sat in Richard's seat, and won his crown after he had laid it by. So you see I should find myself possessed of all historical knowledge through my interest in this daring crusader, whose

6

sword and shield have hung rusted and dull for so many centuries.　　　　　　　　　．

I am convinced, for almost all readers, this is the only way to read history with profit. As well eat when you are not hungry, as read when you are not interested; and, unfortunately, the older histories are dull through their formalism and pedantry, and will only be sought by those born with a passion to know how time has been filled up since the flood.

So the way is to take anybody you care for, and plunge in; the wave that bore him on will sweep you into the current of universal knowledge.

FEAR AS A MOTIVE IN RELIGION.

I WON'T be frightened into being a Christian any way, he said, and put an end to the conversation.

I had heard young people say the same thing before, and had always thought it a piece of foolish bravado suggested by the devil, as the sinner's short cut across convictions crowding the soul a little too closely; but one does not like to say uncomplimentary things always, even when they leap to his tongue for utterance, and so I had been often at a loss how to meet the objection, or rather the *mood* which let such an objection turn the soul away from Christ.

Now I went home and thought about it. "Won't be *frightened* into being a Christian!" Is fear dishonorable to a man, or a boy trying to be a man?

Coward — that *is* a bad word; it cannot be freed from its disreputable associations — but is fear cowardice? the man who is afraid a coward?

There are certainly two things one may fear and still keep his self-respect: danger and wrong.

I ride under some towering top of an Alpine mountain, and just as I am passing I see a huge mass of snow and ice breaking off its frowning front, and I shout to my companions : " Backward, for your lives !" and the avalanche does *not* bury us, nor carry our crushed bodies down the mountain side. Was the fear that blanched my cheek, forced out that warning cry and made me run for my life, a thing to be ashamed of ? No, for the danger was real, and fear natural.

If one congratulates himself on so promptly obeying the instinct of fear in avoiding great personal danger, ought he to be ashamed if he discovers, among the things prompting him to be a Christian, the dangers which threaten his soul if he is not a Christian ? Why is one peril to be avoided and the other to be braved ? Self-respect does not forbid, but commands, that we shun both.

Then there's the fear of wrong ; that is certainly not cowardice. A group of little fellows on the street are planning for coasting on Sunday. Two of them are in doubt about it ; have not been used to that sort of thing ; they are afraid it is wrong. But boy argument and a little expressive contempt soon silence one, and he says : " I'll go ;" but the other holds out, and says finally : " I can't go." Which is the coward ? The boy who dares to do wrong, or the one who is afraid to do wrong ?

A young man stands looking inquiringly at the Christian life. Its self-denials, its duties, its effect upon his companionship, all these things make him afraid of it. And yet he knows and feels the

danger of neglecting God's call to him. While
balancing the two courses, the two sets of motives,
somebody says to him with a solemnity that irri-
tates him: "It is dangerous to delay," or, "This
may be your last chance," and the devil shows him
at once his short cut out of his hesitation, and he
says: "I won't be frightened into religion." But
in turning with a brave air from the fear which
drew him to Christ, and an honorable, manly, safe
Christian life, he is received into the embrace of
another class of fears, which more and more involve
him in self-indulgence, in weakness, in a downward
course of life.

Which set of fears stamp the mark of cowardice
upon him? Fear of wrong is *not* cowardice. It is
only the devil's sophistry which makes it appear so
to ill-taught men. Fear of wrong is the revolt of
our moral nature against immorality; it is the echo
of God's voice in our soul, making us know his
will; but the devil takes this noble fear, and dis-
guises it till it appears, in the consciousness made
murky by selfish purposes already having their
way, as a fear of pain or suffering — against which
it seems an honorable thing in man to rise in resist-
ance. But the man who is not deceived knows
that fear of wrong is God's sentinel put on guard
at the door of his conscience, to keep him from
surrendering his conscience into traitorous hands
and to manacles and chains.

But that fear of danger and fear of wrong are

thus not dishonorable in men, is not all there is to be said in favor of fear as a motive in religion. A close examination of what fear is, shows that it is often love, reverence, faith in crude form ; is to the finer, more exalted emotions of the Christian what pig-iron is to polished steel. Fear is the ore that the thought of God digs out of the untutored human spirit, which knowledge of God shapes into the brighter forms of faith and love. The same things about God that inspire fear, on a better acquaintance, inspire love, faith, trust.

At my examination for entrance to college, I stood in such awe of one of the professors, that when he turned his sharp eyes upon me suddenly and put a simple question to me, I shook with fear, and my tongue absolutely refused to do its office. I came to know him well afterward, in the recitation room, in long walks over the hills, at his table, in his family, and I can see plainly that the same qualites in him which made me fear him once, are precisely what call out the strong respect and affection I now feel for him.

Fear is the tribute weakness pays to strength, littleness to greatness, humility to majesty — but when strength is seen to stoop to help weakness, greatness to condescend to littleness, majesty to woo humility, the first impulse of fear does not so much give way before, as change into, trust and love.

So the strength of God, which to the untaught

soul suggests fear, to the same soul admitted to acquaintance with Him supports confidence; the justice of God, which to the untaught soul suggests terror, to the same soul admitted to acquaintance with Him supports respect; the majesty of God, which to the untaught soul suggests dread, to the same soul admitted to acquaintance with Him supports reverence.

In neglecting the motives to religion which lie in men's fears, there is danger of teaching men want of respect for God. And we can no more love and honor God than a man, without respecting him first. A wholesome fear of God, awakened by right conceptions of His holiness and justice, is the surest introduction to appreciation of His love in Christ. "The secret of the Lord is with them that fear Him "

YUNG WING.

HE first Chinese known to have been in the United States for education were three boys, who were in the short-lived Foreign Mission School at Cornwall, Conn., about the year 1825, and little more can now be learned of them than that they were there.

The next were also a company of three boys, who were brought to this country in 1847 by their teacher, the Rev. S. R. Brown, Principal of the Morrison School at Hong Kong. Their names were Wong Fun, Wong Shing and Yung Wing. They were sent to Monson Academy, and were received into the family of Mr. Brown's mother, who lived in Monson and who is memorable in the church as the author of the hymn: "I love to steal awhile away." It was probably due to their association with this saintly woman, more than to any other means of grace, that there at Monson they all became Christians.

Wong Fun, after three years went, in 1850, to Edinburgh, Scotland, where he graduated in medicine with honor, and whence he returned to China in 1856 to establish himself as a physician in the city of Canton. His professional career was an extraordinary success. He soon became famous, alike for his ability and for his character; he was highly esteemed by all who knew him, and he died in October, 1878, widely regretted. Wong Shing was compelled by ill health to go back to China the year following his arrival in America. Having learned the art of printing in the office of *The China Mail,* he became, in 1852 or 1853, connected with the press of the London Mission at Hong Kong, under Dr. Legge, now of Oxford University, and continued in that employment till quite recently. He is now an official interpreter of the Chinese Embassy to the United States, but for the present on duty with the Chinese Educational Mission at Hartford. He was received a few weeks since into the Asylum Hill Congregational Church in Hartford, on the evidence of credentials which showed that he had been for thirty years a consistent member, and for fifteen years a faithful deacon, of the native church of Christ in Hong Kong.

If Brother Blaine of Maine should chance to be in Hartford, and in the Asylum Hill Congregational Church on a communion Sunday, when Brother Wong Shing chanced to be serving as substitute in the deacon's office at the Lord's Table — an incident not unlikely to occur — he might recognize an occasion for revising and perhaps somewhat qualifying his late verdict respecting the possibility of Chinese evangelization. It was one of Wong Shing's remarks, while Congress was voting that the Chinese must go, that he was very glad that no one would be shut out of Heaven who believed in Christ.

The youngest of the three, Yung Wing, for whom, as events have proved, Divine Providence had marked out so great a work in the future, was the only one who completed his education in this country. He entered Yale College in 1850, the first Chinese student the institution had ever seen. His life in college was full of interest, but cannot here be described. One circumstance that at the time attracted a good deal of attention to him was his twice gaining a prize for English composition. He graduated, with credit, in 1854, and at once sailed for China. It was like going to a strange land. He had been in this country so long that it was home to him. He had nearly forgotten his native tongue. He had become American in his thoughts, tastes, sympathies. He had many friends here, and here he would have dearly loved to spend his life. But he did not consider himself at liberty to do so. His sense of gratitude and of justice forbade it. He felt that his duty was to his own race. He had already formed the plan of the educational mission. It had early become his conviction that the best thing he could do for his country was to procure for other Chinese youths the benefit of the same advantages that he himself had enjoyed. And though he knew not how it was to be brought about, he set his face toward China to wait on what God might there have in store for him.

Sixteen years passed before he accomplished his object. They were years of delay, patient endeavor, frustration, disappointment — of unconquerable perseverance, crowned at last with success.

During the seven years from 1855 to 1862, Yung Wing was, successively, private secretary to the United States Commissioner, law student at Hong Kong, translator in the Customs service at Shanghai, traveling inland agent of a great silk and tea house, and finally for a brief period merchant on his own account. But that which in all these changes he was constantly contriving how to compass, was such an access to persons of public consideration and influence, as would enable him to unfold and advocate his scheme for the education of native youth abroad, to some purpose. It is not easy to appreciate how difficult a matter this was. He had to begin with no *pou sto*, no foothold.

The conditions, in most particulars, were specially unfavorable, much more so twenty years ago than they would be now. But in 1862 he formed the acquaintance of a Chinese scholar of eminence, through whom he was brought to the notice of one of the foremost statesmen of the Empire, the Viceroy Tsang Koh Fan, at that time commander-in-chief of the imperial army and engaged in suppressing the great Taeping rebellion. At an interview to which he was invited with Tsang Koh Fan, at his headquarters in the field, Yung Wing made so favorable an impression upon him, that he was asked to enter the government service. He consented with joy, and our graduate of Yale College became a Chinese mandarin of the fifth rank, there being nine grades of that dignity in the Chinese official system.

Declining the offer of a military command on the score of lack of qualification, he soon after this, in 1864, was dispatched to the United States to purchase the machinery that was the foundation of the Shanghai Arsenal. For the manner in which he discharged this important duty he received his first promotion in rank, which was to the next higher grade, the fourth. He was now in a position to do something for the furtherance of his educational project, and he improved his opportunity to the utmost. He was in frequent intercourse with many of the leading public men of his country, and he never wearied of urging upon their notice the subject that lay nearest his heart. He pleaded, especially, that it was for the interest of China — that it was her obvious necessity — in view of her rapidly extending commercial and political relations, to provide for herself a corps of young men, fitted by foreign residence and study to understand and handle international affairs. He took the patriotic ground that it was impolitic and

unseemly that the public service should be so
largely in the hands of foreigners. But good as
his reasons were, and though he put them forth
with all the enthusiasm of his nature, few had ears
to hear them. There were three men, however,
upon whom he made an impression — all men of
commanding influence. They were the Viceroy
Tsang Koh Fan, already named ; the Viceroy Li
Hung Chang, the same who is now Chinese Prime
Minister, and Ting Yi Tchearg, Governor of the
Province of Kiang Su. Yet impressed and convinced as they were, they shrank from going forward in the matter. The time was not ripe ; the
obstacles were too many ; the risk was too great.

Other years passed, bringing alternations of hope
and fear, but whether encouraged or discouraged,
Wing held to his purpose with unchanging con-
stancy. He often doubted if he should live to see
it achieved, but he never forsook it for one hour.

At last, however, the weary waiting came to an
end, and in a manner that could not have been
anticipated. In 1870, five Chinese representatives,
appointed by the government, met a committee
representing the foreign powers in diplomatic relations with China, to investigate the affair known
as the Tientsin Massacre, which had taken place a
short time before, and to adjust the difficulties
growing out of it. Three of these Chinese representatives — so it came to pass — were the very
three men above named, on whom Yung Wing's

hopes were chiefly placed; and Yung Wing himself was summoned to assist in the business.

The occasion was a most favorable one for striking a blow in behalf of his cause. It happened that the immediate circumstances were of a nature to illustrate and enforce the reasons by which he had hitherto supported it. And its friends were together. Wing perceived the opportunity and seized it. He once more earnestly restated his argument, and begged that steps be taken without delay to carry his views into effect. This time he prevailed. The three great men resolved to act. As the result, in August, 1871, by imperial decree the Chinese Educational Mission became a fact, and Mandarin Yung Wing was the happiest man on the face of the globe. To him the charge of organizing the enterprise was principally committed, and, with another promotion in rank, he was appointed one of the two commissioners entrusted with its establishment and direction in the United States.

It is now seven years since the first detachment of pupils, of whom there have been one hundred and twenty in all, arrived to begin their fifteen years of life and study in America. Some have already entered college; a large number are in our best schools and academies, and all are doing well. Their average of talent is high. It is interesting to remark that in several instances amongst them Yung Wing's success in English composition has already been reproduced, and not a few of them are natural orators. With scarcely an exception their conduct has been not only good, but admirable. Much depends on them; no one can tell how much. Everything is to be hoped for from them. How thankfully and hopefully ought God's people to pray for them.

In December, 1876, Yung Wing was appointed associate minister with Chin Lan Pin, who was for two years co-commissioner with him of the Educational Mission to the United States, Peru and Spain. On this occasion he received his third promotion in rank, viz.: to the second grade, and was invested with the honorary title of Taou Tae (or Intendent) of the Province of Kiang Su. Last autumn he assumed the duties of his new office at Washington, though he still retains a general supervision of the Educational Mission, which it will readily be believed is to him the object of an uncommon affection.

In age, Yung Wing is in the near neighborhood of fifty, though looking much younger. Of medium stature, he is of extraordinary physical strength and activity. Although a Chinese official, he wears, except on occasions of ceremony, the English dress. He speaks English perfectly, with no foreign accent. Under the influence of great excitement, however, he will sometimes mix his words a little. In the summer of 1874 he was ordered by his government to visit Peru, and look into the condition of the Chinese coolies in that country, and thither the writer and another friend accompanied him. By what he heard and saw he was soon filled with burning indignation. One day in the city of Lima, as he was expressing his wrath more openly and freely than, under the circumstances, consisted with prudence, he was remonstrated with, and told that he was putting his life in peril to talk so. Whereupon he hotly replied: "Well, suppose I am! Why shouldn't a man put his life in peril? May be it would be the best use I could make of my life to lay it down right here in Lima! If I thought so, I would do it! *I should have no delicacy about it at all!*" He was assured that, however it might be with him, his companions *did* feel considerable delicacy upon the subject, and wanted more time to consider it.

A man of high, true courage is Yung Wing, and not much afraid of men. When, at the close of this same visit to Peru, he was presented to the President of the Republic, Manuel Pardo, since assassinated, and the President, after an exchange of courteous greetings, said with the confident air of a superior: "Well, Mr. Yung Wing, I trust you haven't found your countrymen so very badly treated amongst us!" Wing replied politely but gravely: "I regret to be compelled to say, Mr. President, that I have found their condition much worse than I had expected, or than had been reported to me;" and in the conversation that followed went on to say to His Excellency a number of most true things concerning the administration of law in Peru, which, however wholesome, it could scarcely have been agreeable to hear; while his friends, it must be confessed, sat out the interview on rather uneasy chairs, and were glad when it was over. Yet Señor Pardo, who was one of the best men Peru ever had, took it all apparently in good part; having, in fact, no reason to do otherwise.

Yung Wing was married in February, 1875, to Miss Mary L. Kellogg, of Avon, Conn., granddaughter on both her father's and her mother's side of Congregational ministers, and the wedding was in the old parsonage where one of them died. Viewing the company assembled, the Chinese friends of the bridegroom in their gorgeous costumes mingled with the other guests; considering, too, the place, an ancient New England village, and the occasion, one could not help wondering what good Parson Kellogg would have thought, if fifty years ago a vision of the scene had passed before him. Two sons are the fruit of this marriage, the elder of whom was baptized Morrison Brown, the first name being that of the first English Protestant missionary to China; and the second one that of the man to whom Yung Wing feels that he personally owes more than to any other.

The giving of these names to his first-born, it will be perceived, eloquently declares his Christian faith and gratitude. That faith he has kept, and it has kept him. It was the source and support of his patience through all those years of trial and hope deferred and lonesomeness in China. It was nothing, he has often told the writer, but his conviction that God had a purpose of good for his country to execute through him, that saved him many and many a time from despair. Again he has said that in his prayers the thing he ever asked was, that in all he did he might play into the plan of God. He is an intense patriot. He loves China. He feels deeply her burdens and her deficiencies and her wrongs. When he considers her wants, he says he wishes that he was a youth again, that he might have a whole life to give to her. He believes in her future; and he believes that that which at last is going to make her the great nation she is capable of being, and is destined to be, is what has given him his manhood — faith in the living God.

GONE!

HE was gone!

The last breath came and went. The gaze was transfixed. The spirit returned to Him who gave it. Tenderly he closed her eyelids, and with breaking heart left the body of his beloved that it might be made ready for burial.

It was a great, great change which her death made in his home. He bore up under it through the excitement of the days which immediately followed the sad event, and then, when the house was again quiet and the old routine of life was resumed, gave way. The sense of loss was almost greater than he could bear.

The "old routine" did I say? There was little or none of the "old." It was all dreadfully new. The light was put out, and the once bright and cheery home was left in darkness. Where was she who used to hang upon his neck when the hour of morning departure came, sending him forth into the world with her sweet breath of blessing?

Gone!

Where was she who watched for his coming step at night, and received him with an embrace which was a refreshment in itself, brushing away with one touch as it were all the encumbrance of care and worry and trial and disappointment with which the day had encrusted him?

Gone!

How the word echoed through the silent house! Gone, and nothing left but the memory of her. Gone, not for a week, nor for a month, nor for a year — what a mercy it would be if he *could* think of her returning in one year, or even in five years, or ten! but no; gone forever. Gone, and all opportunity of love and ministry at an end.

The house remained? Yes; and there were the pictures on the walls, and the books in the book-cases, and the evening paper, damp and fresh. The servants came and went. The fire burned in the grate. The clock ticked on. The body of the once joyous life was all here, but the soul was out of it. And what was the body of that life without its soul?

Poor aching heart! Who could enter into his sorrow? Friends tried to comfort him, but there was little in their comfort. They knew nothing about it. They had never been where he was; they could not put themselves in his place. It was well-meant talk, but idle — their words of consolation. Oh, if the old days could only come back! If he could only take her again, as he had taken her a dozen years before, to love and to cherish, and walk with her once more over the path they had trodden together! If he might only make amends where he had fallen short, and call back what had been repented of, and put unselfishness in place of selfishness, and patience in place of peevishness, and thoughtfulness in place of thoughtlessness! If he could only undo some things he had done, and do some things he had left undone!

But no; she was gone.

And the cry burst from his lips: "Oh God! restore her to me, if it be but for a day!"

"Here I am," said a soft clear voice beside him.

It was *her* voice. He awoke. It had been all a terrible dream.

"The Lord be praised for that!"

"But suppose it had been true?"

And he sat thinking over the possibility. Here she was, the loving and faithful and noble wife, still his to love and cherish. The amends he had dreamed of making he could now make; the things he had left undone he could now do. The lesson which conscience had taught him by an overwrought imagination, he could now apply through the sober medium of fact. And he did. He was a better husband after this — tenderer, gentler, more helpful, forbearing, considerate and kind. The very thought of what might be, moved him with a great power to improve what was.

Are there some homes in which a little parable

like this may come with the force of a mild warning? Are there some husbands, some wives, whom an apparent security in what is, has made a trifle careless as to what may be? This sad word "gone" is being written over one door after another along the way. Some day it will be written over *yours.* Perhaps your turn will come next. If any tear of trembling falls upon this page as you read these words, let it be a tear of contrition for the past and of promise for the future. While she is yet with you, be the husband you pledged yourself to be, and even more. Have you laid a finger's weight of sorrow on that dear and trusting heart? Before the sun goes down lift it off; and never lay such there again.

A TALK WITH GIRLS.

OU are just through school life, or perhaps just finishing. I fear you have graduated five years too early. Young men rarely leave college before they are twenty-three or four, and then their minds are none too mature to comprehend the higher studies, and quite likely you are not over eighteen. If you were asked why you had rushed through school days, which, alas! never come but once, you would not like to say you desired to go into society, or to marry, but the real reason probably is because it is the fashion to leave school in one's teens.

In our school, years ago, there was a young woman of twenty-five, whose scholarly but eccentric father had taught her Greek and Latin, while she knew little of the lower branches. When she came to the seminary, we all treated her as though she were a Feejee Islander. Such foolish pride have girls about remaining in school after they come to sensible years!

After graduation what will you do? If you can be the most useful at home of any place in the world, by all means stay there. A girl rarely appreciates the power she is, or may be, in her home. A sweet voice, a cheery smile, a sunny nature that will not be annoyed at trifles, an unselfish disposition, a desire to minister to others, intelligence that makes one companionable, these are things that make a daughter a joy.

Many girls fret at their mothers. If you had buried yours, as I have mine, and longed again and again for the one person in all the world who forgives everything, and loves through good or ill, you would wish that every word had been the kindest your lips knew how to utter.

Many girls are thoughtless of their fathers, who work all day in office or shop, glad to make any sacrifice, that the daughters may have pretty things for the home or personal adorning. And a caress would have paid these fathers a hundred-fold! Nothing repays labor like love. Strange that we give so little when it makes life so very bright.

Many girls are rude to brothers, who, with a little tenderness, might have been won to the highest respect for womanhood. If they were always as polite to their own as they are to somebody else's brothers, what different households we should often have.

Everybody admired Macaulay as a great essayist and historian, but after his life was written, and the world saw the beautiful devotion between him and his sisters, then everybody *loved* him. The essays of Elia would lose half their beauty did not

Charles Lamb's love for his sister Mary run like a golden thread through all.

Make home so bright, girls, that your brothers will like to remain there evenings. Thousands of boys are ruined by the idle talk and temptations of the street, especially in our cities. If sisters only knew what power they had to lead these eager, restive lads up to noble manhood, they would never fail to use it. Alas, that we realize so many things too late!

Are you helping to share the *burdens* of the home?

I have been in many houses where, if I had not guessed the relationship by the family name, I should have thought the young girls were simply boarders. They sat in the parlor doing fancy work, or receiving friends, or went out for an airing, and let somebody, perchance the mother, do the work.

I know a lovely Christian home where there have been five children, three girls and two boys. One daughter has married, and the other two take entire charge of the house. The mother is cared for as tenderly as though they thought any day God might send for her. She controls her time, does church and benevolent work, and is thankful for such rare children.

Are you learning to sew and to cook?

You will have need for such knowledge, whatever station in life you may occupy. I have a friend who often sorrows over spoiled dinners, and while her husband is very fond of her, he says: "If Hattie only knew about such things, it would make life *so* comfortable!"

I wonder how you look in the early mornings at your own table.

Next to a lovely disposition, nothing influences affection more than neatness. Better wear a clean calico than a dirty silk, on any occasion. The world naturally looks to womanhood for taste and delicacy and neatness, and ought to find it. There is no excuse for an untidy girl, be she rich or poor.

Be prompt in your homes, rising at proper hours, ready at meals, and exact as to appointments. Scarcely anything is more annoying than a person habitually late, and by whom others lose time. Such habits are easily formed and rarely broken, causing irritability everywhere.

Learn to wait upon yourselves. A girl who helps herself is usually helpful to others.

Next to being a Christian, which is above all and includes all — for a woman not to be a Christian is to be a flower without fragrance — next to this, be amiable. You may have the learning of Aspasia, the beauty of Mary Stuart, and the wit of Madam De Staël, but unless your character be lovely, your home will be a failure. A cheerful disposition makes the whole year like a summer morning. Such a girl never gets cross, or answers sharply, passes over little trials, always has a word of encouragement, always a happy smile. In her daily life, she

> "Shows us how divine a thing
> A woman may be made."

FIVE YEARS IN HEAVEN.

FIVE years in heaven, my sweet,
　　And I five years without you —
Years written over to the end
　　With loving thoughts about you;
I wonder are you tall and wise,
　　A woman in your ways,
And do you speak the words out plain
　　In your glad songs of praise?

Is there in heaven, my sweet,
　　An angel like a mother?
And does she hold you very close,
　　And do you kiss each other?
You were a little timid thing,
　　Who scarce had learned to walk,
And clung to gentle mother ways,
　　And tender mother talk.

I think God knows, my sweet,
　　Your need of baby places;
He will not let you droop and pine
　　'Mid grand and dazzling faces.
He gives the little bird a nest,
　　The seed has sunshine duly,
He'll deal with you, my baby girl,
　　As tenderly and truly.

BARONESS BUNSEN.

OON after leaving college, in 1853, I read and re-read Stanley's Life of Dr. Arnold, one of the earliest and one of the greatest works in the new school of biography. In that book I came in contact, for the first time, with the name of the German diplomatist and scholar, Baron Bunsen, or, as he used to be called, the Chevalier Bunsen. Later, in the Life and Letters of Niebuhr, the great historian of Rome, the name of Bunsen came into fresh prominence. A residence in Germany brought the name anew into constant vision and contact, he being daily mentioned as one of the most noted scholars, Christians and statesmen of Europe, known and revered in all Christendom; rising from the estate of a small farmer's son to be the minister of Prussia to Switzerland, Italy and England, the personal and intimate friend of the last king of Prussia and the present Emperor, and one of the first half dozen names, beyond all dispute, in the realm of modern learning, renowned as a Hebrew scholar, as an Egyptologist, as an antiquary, and as a student in hymnology, not to speak of other fields also in which he was eminent.

I well remember that Gov. Wright, formerly
the United States Minister to Prussia, used to
consider it the proudest event of his life that he
had had the privilege of being the guest of Bunsen for a few days. Bunsen died in the winter of
1860, and is buried in the cemetery of Bonn, on
the Rhine, near to Niebuhr the historian, to Arndt
the poet, to Schumann the composer, to Schlegel
the critic, and also near to the wife and son of
Schiller. And it seems but yesterday when, in the
spring of 1865, I stood and looked at the medallion
of that noble head, and read beneath it the words :
" Let us walk in the light of the Eternal."

It was the wife of this great man whose biography is now written by Augustus Hare. She who
had devoted her declining strength to the work of
describing her husband's life, and published that
biography of him which is now well known, and
is in many homes, has herself fallen by the way,
at the advanced age of eighty-five, and in the gentlest and most painless of deaths. I fully assent to
the strong assertion of Mr. Charles Dudley War-
ner, that no biography which has been given to the
world " has the pure charm of this." The flow and
growth of the story would itself eclipse any novel
that has been written ; indeed, no novelist would
hazard so bold an experiment as to make an imagi-
nary life climb up stair by stair to the social hights
which were attained by Baroness Bunsen. And
the book opens out so gradually and so tranquilly,

like the Rhine between Schaffhausen and Bingen, it passes on through such spaces of fruitfulness and peace and household love ; it lets one into the secret of family successes, of the rearing of children, of the making and keeping of friends, of the means of literary, social and religious culture, the uses of adversity, and the uses of prosperity, so sweetly and genially, that, as one closes chapter after chapter, and sees the life widening out, till it is filling Europe with its blessings, one says, surely of all the great, glad gifts which God has made to men, nothing is comparable with such a mother's life, word, spirit, example.

The Baroness Bunsen was the daughter of a plain and untitled English gentleman ; her grandmother having been, however, a maid of honor in the court of George the Third. She was reared in the most careful manner, and went to Rome to perfect her education. She was an accomplished linguist, and the French, Italian and German languages came to be on her lips not less fluent than her mother tongue. She was so accomplished in the arts of drawing and painting, as to call out the praises of Thorwaldsen, then living in Rome at the hight of his great fame. She was an enthusiast in the study of the antiquities of Rome, and made the acquaintance of Bunsen, then a young subordinate in the Prussian legation, but a most competent guide to all that remains of the glories of ancient Rome. The six months' acquaintance

resulted in marriage in 1817; to the eye of the
world the union of two young and noble natures,
full of aspirations after the best and highest culture, as well as after all that is good.

It was the marriage of a Secretary of Legation
to a young English girl of good but not eminent
family; that was all. When one remembers that
the cousin of that young bride is, at this very
moment, the M. Waddington who is the French
Minister of Foreign Affairs, and next to the President the highest official in France; when one turns
to the close of the volume and reads the letter
which the Emperor of Germany wrote her with his
own hand; when one finds her subsequent intimate
relation to Queen Victoria, and to her family, and
to all that is socially and intellectually great in
Germany, the whole atmosphere of the book during
the last two thirds of it, in the very highest social
places of the world; not simply identification with
people nobly born, but with the noblest of the
noble; the visits of kings and princes, and the first
scholars of the world at her house, no more to her
than the calls of common men and women are to
us — one is overwhelmed with the change.

Twelve children were born to the Bunsens; two
died in their infancy, ten came to manhood and
womanhood, and nearly all married, were blessed
with many children, and are now living in England
and Germany, in the same exalted social position
to which they were born. And out of that large

family, not one ever caused one moment's shame
or grief to the parents.   Here is this woman, the
daily companion of princes ; her husband, the larger
part of his life, the Prussian minister to Italy and
to England, she overwhelmed with society duties,
their palace overrun with guests, and yet she drawing from her own revered mother the lessons which
she was giving to her ten children, and so rearing
them that we fail to find in one of them the faint-
est tendencies to go astray.   And yet with it all,
Madame Bunsen remains just a woman ; just what
Wordsworth described his own wife to be.

If one were to compare the living of Baron Bunsen with that of his wife, he would discover that
there is no power which is working upon the world
to transform it like that of sanctified womanliness.
There was Bunsen, a great scholar, a great states-
man, a great Christian, not ten men in the world
where he lived who stood before him in any one of
these roles ; there was his wife, who shared all his
studies, all his honors, all his friendships, and yet in
her there is a certain strong, persuasive, pure, delicate somewhat, which makes her letters peculiar,
and gives them a certain cleansing power, so that
after you have read them you feel as if you had
come out of a bath.

The way in which her heart follows her children
wherever they go, the way in which she seeks to
stand between them and all peril, and all wrong,
the way in which she seeks to carry over her

experience to them, and to cover them with her love and care, is a delightful suggestion of Him of whom we read that, having loved His own, He loved them to the end. Womanliness is a great thing — a wonderful thing; even perverted womanliness is an amazing thing, as I was thinking a few weeks ago while reading Mary Wolstonecroft's letters, so sad, so tragic, wrung out of a sore, baffled and weary life; but sanctified womanliness, that where the love, purity, duty, devotion of a noble woman are ennobled by what is the gift of Jesus Christ, this is the highest and the best thing on earth. It is the most radiant force in the world. It is that which brings Jesus the nearest to men.

C

WILL SMITH'S ADVENTURE.

ILL Smith was as smart a boy as there was in all Sweetwater.   He was the son of one of the Gettysburg heroes, and his mother —a very hard-working woman — spared no pains to make her little boy industrious and honest, a worthy son of a worthy father. Among the virtues which she impressed upon his mind was that of self-reliance ; to be manly, independent and decisive in action.   His habits of industry were very marked.   He was always ready to do anything by which he could earn something to aid his mother, and the early passengers for the cars always found him ready to carry their trunks to the depot in the town.   He was an excellent hand with a snowshovel, also, and the snow seemed to favor him, during the season of it, for it would come down in the night, and Will would be out by daylight with his shovel pitching into the drifts before the neighbors' houses, who would pay him handsomely for his work.   There was considerable competition in the snow-shoveling business, but he would be up so early that he led all the rest.   He was very faithful and exact in doing errands, and won the

"And the early passengers for the cars always found him ready to carry their trunks to the depot."   Page 114.

reputation of being a first-class boy. Indeed, he was "first-class" in school and everywhere, and Mrs. Smith was proud of her son.

And yet, he was only a "human boy" — not so good as to run the risk of his dying very soon on that account, as some people think good boys are liable to. He played as heartily as the best; enjoyed vacations, and wished that they might come often ; loved mischief as well as any other boy, if there were no malice in it ; could jump, run, climb, swim, skate, coast, play base ball, cricket, kick foot-ball, and do anything that a boy of his size and age could do. He would never quarrel, and, somehow or other, occasions for quarreling were very rare where he was. If, at any time, differences occurred, as they will in the dealings of boys or men, Will, though but twelve years old, had an influence that was felt among his associates, and he would soon make all straight and smooth again. There was a time, however, when he got drawn into a quarrel with Ted Halsey, by a man who should have been in better business, and they came to blows; but Ted whipped him. Will said he had rather it would be so, and Ted and he were fast friends thereafter. It is a very mean thing for men or big boys to set little boys to fighting, who ought to be always loving and kind towards each other ; though oftentimes they are not, but have their "spats," and act very much as men do when they are angry. It is the bad part of manhood in the bud.

But the story I have to tell has little in it to which any of the qualities I have named as Will's will apply. It rather reveals a new quality which I have not named — judgment.

He had been out one morning early, on some errand, and was going home to his breakfast, when a lady opened the front door of her house hurriedly, and looked anxiously down the street. Will, attracted by her manner, turned round and looked in the same direction.

"Little boy," said she, "did you meet a gentleman walking towards the depot, wearing a light coat and carrying a heavy cane?"

"Yes, ma'am," replied Will; "a big man, walking very fast."

"Do you think you could overtake him?"

"I'll try."

"Well, then, take this pocket-book that he has left behind him, and which is very important to him, and if you can overtake him and give it to him, I will give you half a dollar on your return."

Will took the pocket-book, and started upon the run for the depot. The moment he was gone, the lady remembered that she had not asked his name nor residence. The book, containing money and notes, was very valuable, and she had entrusted it to an entire stranger. She was in an alarming state of anxiety about it, and waited impatiently for the return of the boy. After waiting an hour

or two, and finding that he did not come, she concluded that he had made off with the money, and
went to the chief of police to report her loss. She
described the boy as well as she could, and the
officers were sent out in search of him.

Will started from the lady's door in the hurry I
have described, and arrived at the depot just as the
train was moving. He made up his mind in an
instant. He was on the side of the train opposite
to the depot, by which a platform ran, and, seizing
the rail, he swung himself on and went with the
car, no one at the depot having seen him.

" Hallo, little fellow ! " said the brakeman ; " you
came near getting left."

" That's so," replied Willie, laughing.

He went into the car, which was about the first
one, and then went through the train until he
reached the very last one before he saw the gentleman of whom he was in search. As he stood by
the seat in which the person sat, he heard him
lamenting to the gentleman with him the acci-
dental leaving of his pocket-book behind him, at
the house of his sister in Sweetwater, and the
absence of papers needed by him at the place
where he was going, which were in that book. The
court was to be in session that day, and a cause in
which he was interested would have to be delayed
in consequence.

" I would give," said he, " a hundred dollars to
have that book."

"Can't you telegraph back at the next station, and have it sent on?" asked the other gentleman.

"No, the next train does not leave till two, and it would be impossible to reach me in season. Bad! All my journey of sixty miles is for nothing, besides the annoyance of the delay."

Will gently touched the gentleman's arm, and he, probably thinking it was some pedlar boy, rudely threw the little hand off, when, after a moment's hesitation, Will held the pocket-book before the eyes of its owner. Much surprised, he gazed at it a moment as if in doubt as to what it was, then eagerly grasped it and looked round at the little fellow who had presented it. Will had a sly humor, and his eye sparkled at the fun of the thing.

"Where did you find this?" the gentleman said.

"Didn't find it, sir," said Will. "A lady gave it to me and told me to run and give it to you at the cars."

"And why didn't you give it to me at the cars?"

"Because the cars had already started when I got there, sir, and as the lady told me that it was important you should have it, I jumped on to overtake you."

The gentleman opened the pocket-book, as if to satisfy himself that the contents were all right, and then asked:

"Were you not going on with the train?"

"No, sir; my only business was to find you."

" And how do you expect to get back ? "

" Never thought of that, sir."

" Well, we must take care of you at Centerport, and as I shall return to-morrow, I will take you with me."

Then the gentleman turned to his companion and left little Will to his reflections. He had, indeed, thought of nothing but restoring the pocket-book, and now the reflection came to him that his mother would be very anxious regarding his absence ; but he argued to himself that the time would be very short before he would see her again ; and so, with a boyish love of adventure inspiring him, and the consciousness of having performed a good act, he sat still and let matters take their own course. By and by the gentleman questioned him regarding his circumstances, and his questions were answered in such a straight-forward, manly way, that both gentlemen were delighted with him. His fare was paid to the conductor, and when the lunch-boy came in Will well made up for his lost breakfast.

When the train reached Centerport, which is a large city, a carriage was taken for the best hotel in the place, and Will was at once introduced to the first society. He felt very strangely, but improved his time in seeing the many new things that presented themselves ; yet the thought of his mother would disturb him, and he was not sorry, the next morning, to find himself on the road to

Sweetwater. Every boy who has been away from home, for ever so little while, can tell how pleasant it is to come back to it. Every object is seen with a new interest, and even trees and bushes and rocks seem like dear friends. So Will was very happy when he saw the steeples of Sweetwater over the trees, and thought how glad his mother would be to welcome him back.

A terrible sensation was caused in Sweetwater by Will's mysterious absence. His mother was about frantic, and had set all her friends to search for the missing boy, who met, very soon, the police in search for him, on complaint of stealing the pocket-book. This nearly broke her heart. It was the saddest news she had heard since the day succeeding the battle in which his father fell; shame for his dishonesty being added to pain at his loss, and she felt as if she could not be comforted.

As Will stepped upon the platform, in advance of his friend the owner of the pocket-book, who stopped a moment to bid the other gentleman good-by, a man with a blue coat and brass buttons and a cap marked with a brass figure, took Will by the arm:

"Ah! my young friend," said he, "we've been looking for you. Didn't expect you back quite so soon, though."

"What have I done?" asked Will, as white as paper.

"Done! why run away with a pocket-book, to be sure."

Will was too full of amazement to make a reply, and the people standing round, seeing his scared look, set it down as direct evidence of guilt. The gentleman here stepped from the car and sternly demanded of the officer what he was troubling that boy for?

"'Rested him for robbery," the man replied; "stole a pocket-book. Come along," to Will.

"But the pocket-book was mine," said the gentleman, "and he placed it in my hands."

"Can't help it," returned the officer; "law is law, and a writ is a writ. He must go before the Marshal."

"Well, I will go with him."

Getting into the carriage they drove to the City Marshal's office, and there Mr. Grovenor, the owner of the book, stated the facts in the case, and showed the pocket-book; but Will's discharge was not given until Mrs. Christie, the complainant, had been sent for to release the complaint. She came, and the matter was soon adjusted. She was a nervous woman, had imagined the worst, and was very sorry that she had employed the police. They both drove with Will to his mother's house, and the change in her feelings from sorrow to joy was almost too much to bear. Her boy was safe and innocent, for which she devoutly thanked God, and she listened well pleased to the praise which Mr. Grovenor bestowed upon him.

"And now," said he, "I will do what I promised.

I said I would give a hundred dollars for the possession of that book, and here it is," placing a one hundred dollar greenback in Will's hand.

The boy did not wish to take it, but his new friend said he must do so, as the service he had done was worth much more than that to him. And this was not all. Mrs. Christie became his warm friend, and the presents that he received were many and valuable.

Mr. Grovenor also told him that when he was a little older he would give him a business direction, which he has since done, and Will promises to become prominent as a business man.

BE NOT A JACK-AT-ALL-TRADES.

HE gospel of *thoroughness!* Has it not been preached in our country from the days of poor Richard down to the days of poor Horace? But what work the Yankee nation makes in its practice! What flimsy railway bridges; what frontier cookery; what dabblings in science; what hybrid styles in architecture, what mush — and what mummy cerements — in theology; what rickety chairs and bedsteads; what combustible cities; what colossal ignorance of political economy in Congress! Doing things thoroughly is not the distinguishing national characteristic. But in the confidence with which he turns his hand to anything, the American has no rival.

There is our old friend Off hand. When he was fifteen he left the village academy, to learn the machinist's trade. Business was brisk, and in a year and a half he was taken into another shop as a journeyman. At nineteen he married, and his father-in-law gave him an interest in his drug-store. In due time he dubbed himself " Dr." in the advertisements of his wonderful Siberian cough caramels. In two or three years he traded his patent

medicine business for a printing office, started a
newspaper, and wrote editorials on the Eastern
Question. When the war broke out, he raised an
artillery company, on the strength of his experience as a machinist, and took the field as its cap-
tain. His first campaign developed an unsuspected
weakness of the lungs, and he obtained an assign-
ment to duty as a provost-marshal in Maryland.
Failing in his attempt to get a brevet appointment
as brigadier-general, he resigned his commission
and secured a place as examiner in the Patent
Office. Thrown out of this berth after a while, he
organized a company to work a lead mine in Mis-
souri, and became the secretary of a coöperative
life insurance association which had a desk in the
same office in Chicago. Both companies were so
soon done for, that no one ever knew what they .
were begun for, and he started a restaurant on the
next street.

Since then he has had some ups and more downs.
He has been a market gardener, a school teacher,
a real estate agent, and a lay preacher. If he were
one or two grades lower in the social scale, he
would probably take his turn as a tramp. He
occasionally drops into a current that carries him
along to a temporary business success, in spite of
his inexperience and incapacity. But in such a
case he never knows enough to get out of the
current before it flows back and takes his gains
along with it. He usually does business on

credit. He has to. If by chance he comes into possession of a little capital, he is very likely to fall into the toils of that sort of man who said of his new and unskilled partner : " He puts in the capital and I put in the experience. When we dissolve, I shall have the capital and he will have the experience." He is a good fellow, and has no little ability. The mistake of his life has been in supposing that a man can earn a workman's wages, without serving a workman's apprenticeship.

The conditions of life in a new country, where opportunities are abundant, where competition is less close, where everything floats on a rising tide — conditions that, however, are slipping away from us year by year — greatly stimulate this jack-at-all-trades tendency. In the Old World they have learned a better way. When one must spend seven years in learning a trade, he is apt to stick to it. When fluctuations in prices are so slight that there is no temptation to commercial gambling, and the margin for profits is so small that every economy must be skillfully studied, the novice or the adventurer stands a poor chance; thoroughness becomes the inexorable condition of success.

Rev. Dr. Taylor, of New York, in some newspaper notes of one of his trips across the Atlantic, has alluded incidentally to the experience of a young man who was a member of his former congregation in Liverpool. He was the son of a

wealthy manufacturer, who was engaged in making
the machinery for steamships. As a part of his
preparation for becoming a member of the firm and
a manager of the business, he obtained an appointment as sixth assistant engineer on an Atlantic
steamship ; glad, for the sake of becoming thoroughly familiar with the practical workings of the
machinery, to shut himself up in the bilge-water
smells, the grease, the foul air and the cramped
quarters of a subordinate in the bowels of a
tumbling steamer — a life as near like Jonah's in
the whale's belly as anything that could be imagined. It was characteristic of English thoroughness. It sometimes happens, but it is not the rule,
that the young American who is born to a fortune,
and who is heir-apparent to the business by which
it was built up, ties himself down to drudgery in
just that way. He feels the need of being free for
a hunting trip to Canada, or a sleighing party on
the avenue, or surf-bathing at Cape May, as occasion offers. When the business falls to him, he
depends on his foreman to run it; and when the
next generation comes on the stage, the foreman's
sons are the proprietors, and *his* boys are beating
about the bush to get a living the best way they
can.

Every recurrence of hard times strands a multitude of men, who, simply because they are not
masters of any trade or profession, are as helpless,
for the time being, to get a livelihood, as a turtle

on his back. Every reader will recall such acquaint-
ances — men and women for whom his heart aches
whenever he meets them in these dull times. But
the times never get so hard that the best salesman
in the store, the best mechanic in the shop, the
best lawyer in the county, the best printer in
the office, the best doctor in the town, the best
pastor in the conference, finds himself for any
length of time thrown out of work. The best man,
though, is never the man who has picked up his
trade — who is half carpenter and half farmer,
sometimes preacher and sometimes music teacher,
to-day grocer's clerk and to-morrow car-driver.
He is not a jack-at-all-trades.

There are many things to be learned from these
hard times. But there certainly is a special
message in them for parents and young people.
They say to every young man, especially : *Choose
some useful way of earning your own living;
master it, and stick to it.* Then you will be prepared to escape the worst evils of hard times, and
reap the best fruits of good times.

BAD BOOKS.

———

HE chief danger to young readers lies in their tendency to choose their reading altogether from among works of fiction; and it is to be feared that the number of bad books read at an age when the mind is most impressible, will always be greater than the number of good ones. I use the term *bad books* with intention, although I do not mean books always positively bad in moral teaching. I know most excellent fathers and mothers who would be shocked to hear that there were any bad books admitted into their families, whose children have never read a really good book in their lives. A book is truly a bad book, when it is utterly worthless; when it contains nothing to enrich the memory or feed the mind, leaving both thought and memory poorer from the draught on them; which fatigues without planting any seed there. Such books are found everywhere, in public libraries, circulating libraries, and Sunday school libraries as well. Indeed I have seen some books from some of the Sunday schools which were hardly less questionable in their teaching than in their use, or misuse, of the English tongue, and which the discriminating critic would throw away as unfit for the place they occupy.

It would be absurd to urge that one should never read for amusement. Often the mind is tired with study or other mental strain, and needs rest and recreation as the body needs it, and sometimes finds it in the pages of a wholesome story. The chief anxiety is, that among young people especially, and largely among women, stories are the almost universal reading. It is like constantly feeding the stomach on sugar plums, this keeping the mind always fed on fiction. Mental dyspepsia is as certain in the one case as physical dyspepsia in the other. After a time nothing wholesome will digest, and the mind loses all taste for good fare. If the muscle is not used, it grows flaccid and flabby for want of exercise ; so the mind which is never set to work on anything that arouses and stimulates its powers, and makes it firm and substantial, becomes nothing but an inert and flabby mass, incapable of generating airy ideas and completely useless as a thinking-machine.

It is sad to reflect how all this trash, constantly falling into the hands of young people tends, by its sensational character, to draw them away from better books, which they would relish if their tastes were not spoiled by the higher-seasoned fare which is served up daily and almost hourly from the printing-presses. When one looks over the lists of

cheap periodicals, newspapers and magazines, that
our boys and girls, and young men and women,
devour in weekly and monthly issues ; when he
reads the sensational stories, illustrated by pictures
that disgrace art, the healthy mind is sickened
and disgusted. The printing-press, instead of
appearing a blessing to the human race, assumes
the shape of a monster, which spawns its brood of
hideous crawling things into the purest channels
of life, poisoning and infecting the very well-
springs of existence. When one looks through the
columns of some of these abortions of the press,
one is inclined to believe that those who write this
mass of harmful rubbish should be punished in the
same manner as those other wretches who are
caught putting poison into wells of sweet water,
or mixing arsenic in wholesome bread-stuffs. Has
any one who reads this article ever examined a
pile of some of the weekly newspapers for boys
and girls published in this country, or even some
of those reprinted from English publications?
Has he seen the stories for boys, with their charac-
ters of impossible Indians, of highly-colored hunt-
ers and trappers, of boy heroes, runaways from
home or from school, engaged in all kinds of pre-
posterous adventures, the whole infected with most
questionable sort of teaching, and all written in a
slang almost incomprehensible to ears unused to it?
Week after week and month after month, these
same ingredients are put into the same machine

which grinds out over and over this jumble of unreality, false teaching, and bad English. And all this time there are books gathering dust on library shelves, unread year after year, that are filled with tales of thrilling adventures, deeds of noble daring, records of sublime heroism, which have the merit both of being true, and of being written in the speech that Shakespeare spoke, and not the mongrel tongue current in the alleys and slums of our large cities.

There are even worse books for our girls and young women than the sort of stuff written to catch the fancy of our boys. These are the trashy sentimental novels, as silly and as unlike reality as the boys' stories of adventure. Without saying anything against the morality of these books, which is often open to severest criticism, they inculcate false ideas of human life, present distorted views of character, and fill the mind with a sickly sentimentality, which is a most pernicious preparation for the duties of life that awaits the woman. Is it not the severest possible criticism on the young women of our cities, that in nine cases out of ten such books as those I have indicated are those they select for their chief reading? Such stories circulate from our libraries, rather than the really noble works of fact, fiction or poetry. The young woman whose ideas have been derived from such books as these, enters upon life as unprepared for its requirements as the fledgeling who is tumbled from the parent nest before it has learned to spread its wings. The bitter mistakes from which so many suffer the consequences, the sad awaking to life's realities, might be spared many young souls if their reading were carefully advised and overlooked by those who have charge of their mental training.

To the neglect or indifference of fathers and mothers is much of this careless reading due. They are often ignorant of the books which are in the hands of their children; they neither know nor inquire what is the chief staple of the mental food they are drawing from books and newspapers, outside the usual routine of the text-books used in school. The tender mother who makes the comfort and elegance of her daughter's dress the object of weightiest consideration, is often entirely ignorant of that which shall clothe her daughter's mind. When parents shall show the same care in reviewing what their children read that they show in the provision for their stomachs, or the supervision of their wardrobes, the whole nation will reap the fruits of such care. For a race of cultured and thoughtful men and women will arise, whose minds, generously nurtured by the best books, will direct a noble republic, founded on the intelligence of its children.

THE OTHER SIDE OF THE MOON.

SHE turns her great grave eyes toward mine,
  While I stroke her soft hair's gold;
We watch the moon through the window shine;
  She is only six years old.
" Is it true," she asks, with her guileless mien,
  And her voice in tender tune,
" That nobody ever yet has seen
  The other side of the moon?"

I smile at her question, answering " yes ; "
  And then, by a strange thought stirred,
I murmur, half in forgetfulness
  That she listens to every word :
" There are treasures on earth so rich and fair
  That they cannot stay with us here,
And the other side of the moon is where
  They go when they disappear !

" There are hopes that the spirit hardly names,
  And songs that it mutely sings ;
There are good resolves, and exalted aims ;
  There are longings for nobler things ;
There are sounds and visions that haunt our lot,
  Ere they vanish, or seem to die,
And the other side of the moon (why not ?)
  Is the far bourn where they fly !

" We could guess how that realm were passing sweet,
　　And of strangely precious worth,
If its distant reaches enshrined complete
　　The incompleteness of earth !
If there we could find, like a living dream,
　　What here we but mourn and miss,
Oh, the other side of the moon must beam
　　With a glory unknown in this ! "

" Are you talking of Heaven ? " she whispers now,
　　While she nestles against my knees.
And I say, as I kiss her white, wide brow,
　　" You may call it so, if you please . . .
For whatever that wondrous land may be,
　　Should we journey there, late or soon,
Perhaps we may look down from Heaven and see —
　　The other side of the moon ! "

CRITICISM OF REVIVALS.

A N incident in the life of Aaron Burr illustrates the need of a *balanced* judgment of those phenomena which often perplex good men in revivals of religion. Revivals, whatever else they are, are profound agitations of human passions. The depravity of man is stirred to its depths, and the wiles of Satan are tasked to use it to the worst. Good and evil, God and Satan, come then into visible and extreme conflict. It is no marvel that in the heat of the excitement, great truths should become entangled with great errors. To distinguish wisely the Divine, the human, and the Satanic, in such scenes, is no easy matter.

Good men have therefore been divided in opinion respecting almost all the great historic revivals which have agitated the church. This has been especially true in our American history. We have but to mention the names of Edwards, Whitefield, Tennent, Nettleton, Finney, for illustration. These men were all "withstood to the face" by men as good. Churches were warned against their teachings. Ecclesiastical authority was invoked against some of them. Religious inquirers were cautioned against their " fanaticism."

This last fact is the one which the incident referred to in the life of Burr illustrates. · A revival of great power occurred while he was in Princeton College. It was in his senior year — the period in which the approach of the responsibilities of manhood has been blessed of God to the conversion of so many educated men. Burr acknowledged his interest in the movement which had roused his companions. He confessed that he felt the weight of his godly ancestry upon his conscience. As the son of parents of illustrious piety, he was appealed to by the friends of the revival to give his heart to Christ.

With what degree of wisdom he was approached cannot now be known. The revival, like others of that age, was doubtless not free from some objectionable features. The theology of the age was not a well-balanced theology. The usages of the pulpit were not well-rounded. Appeals to the fears of men were disproportionate to the preaching of the milder aspects of the gospel. It was an age, also, of revolutionary awakenings. The political eloquence of those times shows that profound passions were stirring in the popular heart. They were soon to break out in bloodshed. It is not unphilosophical that religious awakenings should have taken some coloring from the political indignations underneath. Yet those awakenings may have been none the less the work of God, for that.

Then, as so often before and since, good men stood committed to and against the revival. Their prayers met clashing in the upper air, like those two cannon balls from opposing ranks which are said to have struck each other in one of the battles of the Wilderness in our civil war. Especially did the New England and the Scotch theologies stand in battle array on opposite sides. Dr. Witherspoon, then President of Princeton College, a Scotchman by birth, and his countrymen generally, were in opposition to the leaders of the movement. They could see only the human and the Satanic elements, where other good men could see only the mighty hand of God.

Unfortunately, it was to the venerable president that Burr went with the inquiries of his quickened conscience. Up to that time he had not abandoned, nor grossly dishonored, his inherited beliefs. He revered the faith of his illustrious father, and more illustrious grandfather, the elder Edwards. He spoke with tears of the piety of his mother. To human judgment it would appear that he, above all others, should have been one of the converts in that revival. Then, it should seem, was the probable turning point in his life. It is not improbable that his salvation then hung suspended in a trembling balance. It was a crisis in which his religious adviser needed to weigh well his every word, and with prayer. It was no time for sweeping judgments or theologic niceties of schoolmen.

Dr. Witherspoon unqualifiedly condemned the excitement which, he said, was then "raging" in the college. He told Burr that it was all "fanaticism," that it was "wildfire," and that it would soon die out. Specially he taught his trusting pupil, that an educated man should not permit his mind to be agitated by such scenes. We can readily imagine the positive and severe terms in which a man like Dr. Witherspoon, the lineal descendant of John Knox, and as honest as he in his life-long convictions, would be likely to *heap* upon the movement his denunciations and his scorn.

Burr's biographer tells the result of the interview in the few words: "he went away relieved." Relieved of what? As the event proved, he was relieved of his awakened conscience, relieved of his convictions of sin, relieved of his aspirations after a higher life, relieved of the strivings of God's spirit. It is not known that he ever again was profoundly awakened to the worth and the peril of his soul. On that subject he became a very silent man. So far as his life discovered to observers the secret workings of his mind, he never again approached so near to Heaven. Then began the downward career, in which he abandoned the faith of his youth, alienated himself from the church of his fathers, deliberately stepped out of the line of a godly inheritance, and gave up a spiritual birthright such as few other men ever had. In a little more than thirty years from that time he was a murderer. Who can say that the catastrophe of that ruined life was not due, in part, to those sweeping denunciations by Dr. Witherspoon of that religious awakening. In that revival, whatever else was true of it, some men of intelligence and culture were converted, who became shining lights in the church and ornaments to her ministry. Who shall in the last day give answer to the question : "Why was not Aaron Burr one of them ?"

Men need to be very humble, and very docile, when they are called on to pass judgment upon a great quickening of the popular mind, which *may* be the work of God. God moves sometimes in eccentric curves. He condescends to use eccentric instruments. He speaks by semi-pagan prophets like Balaam ; and, for the want of a better apostle, by Balaam's ass. He is not repelled by the vagaries of the minds he has to deal with. He does not abandon the field of conflict, in offended dignity, because "Satan comes also." Why should we judge by tests more fastidious than His ? There is a way of "trying the spirits whether they be of God," which will not commit us to a wrong, nor put to hazard a right. It is a way thronged by prayers, and trodden by docile inquirers, who are ever saying to themselves : "Who hath directed the Spirit of the Lord ; or, being His counselor hath taught Him ?"

ZOÖLOGICAL GARDENS AT NINEVEH AND BABYLON.

THESE cities were built on a magnificent scale, and were adorned with parks, gardens, artificial lakes and fountains, to an extent far beyond any ordinary conception. We learn, from the inscriptions that have been recovered from the sites of those cities, many facts with regard to the skill displayed in ornamenting their public grounds, and the methods employed for making the suburbs of their large towns attractive and beautiful. By royal command the streets must be of a certain width, and the houses must be at a specified distance from the street. One avenue of unusual width and beauty was called "King Street." Public squares in a city are often mentioned, and sometimes the great gate of the city opened into a large and beautiful park. Sometimes these parks bordered on the river, along which ran paved walks, overhung by trees, and provided at intervals with seats for the accommodation of the public, which were generally protected by awnings. In that hot climate such awnings would be needed, even where the walks and seats were shaded by trees. The banks of the river were farther ornamented in such a way as to make them delightful places for promenades. Some of these walks and avenues were lined with figures of lions, and bulls, and other animals, and here and there were shrines of some gods and goddesses, all of which were arranged and kept in repair by royal command.

Special care was also bestowed upon their public gardens. Sometimes these were of such extent that they could be called plantations, where gardens, lakes, fruit-trees, orchards and forests were combined in one royal park. The work of planting trees in such places is often mentioned, both shade and fruit-trees; also choice plants and vines; and, in fact, trees, shrubs and plants from distant countries were brought at the public expense and planted on the banks of the Tigris and the Euphrates, and cultivated by skilled laborers; and over such gardens was appointed a special overseer, as much as there was over the public treasury. A special feature connected with such gardens were the artificial lakes, the fountains, and the flowing streams. Such luxuries existed and are frequently mentioned; although they must have been provided at great expense. Where the fountains are referred to we sometimes meet with the phrase: " Jets of water glistening in the sun." In these ponds or lakes were kept many kinds of fish and birds.

This leads me to speak of the *menagerie parks*,

with which many of the large cities were furnished. These, also, were maintained at the public
expense. In connection with the public grounds
already mentioned, or sometimes separate from
them, were large zoölogical gardens, which, although
they existed ten and eleven centuries before Christ,
were, nevertheless, equal to some of the finest that
are to be seen in our day. Here were collected
animals from all parts of the world. Whenever a
king made a campaign to some remote country, he
brought back with him a supply of animals for his
menagerie. Conquered kings would frequently send
such animals as a free-will offering. These animals
and birds were arranged in suitable apartments or
cells, and over each was written the name and
country to which the particular animal belonged.
It is a curious fact that in a few cases they wrote
over the cell: "The name of this animal is not
known." In these collections rare, curious and
beautiful animals, birds and fish were to be
found. They speak of collecting these animals
from "mountain and plain, from river and sea, from
lands and waters at the ends of the world." We
know that fish were brought from the Mediterranean, and animals from Armenia, Arabia and
Egypt.

Large numbers of these wild beasts, such as
bulls, buffaloes, tigers and lions, were kept apart
from the others for the purposes of the chase; for
the kings from first to last were passionately fond

of hunting. As many as fifty lions were brought at a time and confined in these pens or "dens," and used for the purpose just named. Of course these animals must be fed, and state criminals like Daniel could thus be turned to good account. At the same time, being destroyed in this manner, as Daniel's persecutors were, was a most terrible punishment.

Every child knows that Daniel was cast into the den of lions; but few, perhaps, whether children or adults, have ever had it explained to them *what the lions were there for.* Some, also, have innocently supposed that Daniel was taken to the mountains, or to a great distance, where a lion's den existed, and there cast in among the wild beasts as described in the Bible. The "den," however, was near at hand, either within the city limits or in the suburbs. It should be remembered, further, that there were not three or four or half a dozen lions, merely, in this den, but scores, and probably hundreds, of them, which would make the thought of being cast into such a place all the more terrible, and enhance the greatness of the miracle of his preservation. The enclosures were surrounded by high walls, and the entrances were artificial, and must not be thought of as a natural hole in a ledge of rocks.

WHO WAS MRS. BEARDSLEY'S NEIGHBOR?

HEN Mrs. Beardsley went to Dalton to live, she knew very few people. She had lived in a city all her life, been educated well, and came of a cultivated and rather proud family; but she was not proud in their fashion. She had always earned her own living in one way or another, chiefly by writing for magazines and newspapers. Whatever the outside world may think, this is not a lucrative business, and our friend had other people to help on in life, so she had laid up nothing; and after a while she married a poor man and came to Dalton, a flourishing country town, to live. They went to housekeeping in an old house, small and inconvenient, but of pleasant outlook, and, once settled, began to look about them. "Oh, Fred! I do hope I shall have nice neighbors," said the little woman as they sat at breakfast one day.

"I don't know, Tina, how you'll like them; of course they'll like you."

"That's very proper of you to say, sir," laughed Mrs. Beardsley, "but I'm more apt to like people than they are to like me."

This was quite true. Justina Beardsley was very honest, frank, unconventional and acute ; she spoke her mind too freely to be always a comfortable friend. Human nature loves flattery, and she never flattered ; however, our business is with her neighbors.

Up the street lived the Dean family. Mrs. Dean was a handsome, cool, calm sort of woman, with three daughters, all under fourteen. Her husband kept a country store and had made some money ; her house was very fine with shining furniture, Brussels carpets, and always strictly curtained, screened, and blinded from sun and air. Mrs. Dean was a very good woman ; she never failed to attend every meeting there was, and she always went to church, rain or shine, and took her children to Sunday school with the same persistence. She was a woman who did her duty in these respects earnestly and conscientiously, and never could understand why every one else was not equally faithful.

Now her new neighbor was not a strong woman, and her work was hard. It frequently happened to her to have a dreadful neuralgic headache on Sunday, and though she was accustomed in her youth to go to church as punctiliously as the minister himself, and had really overworked herself in the city mission Sunday schools, she frequently now spent the day of rest on her sofa, with throbbing pangs in her head, and a back aching in every fiber. Nor did she send Tommy, her little five year old boy, to Sunday school; for she preferred to teach him at home.

"Have you been to see Beardsley's wife, my dear?" said Mr. Dean one morning, about three weeks after the new neighbors made their appearance.

"No, not yet. I thought I should not hurry. I do not think she is a very good person to be intimate with. She does not send her boy to Sabbath school, and hardly ever goes to church. I should not wish to encourage such a person to visit us freely."

Mr. Dean said no more. His wife's chin was square, and her lips thin; he really respected her rather severe goodness. She did call on the new comer; was a little horrified to find what common furniture she had, and how the sun streamed in on the old three-ply carpet; and she went away leaving behind her a chill such as follows an iceberg. Mrs. Beardsley knew she was disapproved of, and why, for she was quick of discernment; and knowing inwardly that she really did try and wish above all things to be a Christian woman, she felt sad and sorry that her light did not shine better. Then it occurred to her that, after all, God knew about it, and knew she did like to go to church, and did not like to be kept at home with neuralgia and exhaustion, so she left this new trouble to Him. Down the street lived Mrs. Roberts, a well-to-do mechanic's wife.

"I see Beardsley's folks have moved in," was her husband's comment.

"Yes, they have; but I shan't trouble them with my company. She's a city woman, and writes for the papers besides. She won't want to see common folks like me. Mrs. Dean will call on her, I presume to say, and the rich folks up town; but I know enough not to go where I ain't wanted, and, moreover, I never did like stuck-up folks."

"I don't know but what you're just as good as she is, Mariar; and if you come to the money p'int on't, I could buy an' sell Fred Beardsley over and ag'in."

"Well, I guess you could; but she's got her own click, and I shan't trouble her. I believe in lettin' folks alone, if they feel too smart for your kind. I never did push in where I wa'n't wanted, and I ain't going to begin now."

So Mrs. Roberts stayed away, strenuously held her parasol to the east if her new neighbor was that way, although the sun blazed toward the west, and passed by on the other side. Mrs. Beardsley comprehended the matter, and laughed softly; she would sometime undertake Mrs. Roberts, she thought, and convert her to her own theory of neighborhood; but that time had not come yet.

Next to Mrs. Dean lived Mrs. Morris; she was a pleasant, energetic, talkative person; an indefatigable church-goer, and a benevolent soul; but she did not belong to the Blank church, and the Beardsleys did; she went to the Blanker house of worship, and did not care about any other denomination. It did not afflict her much that Mrs. Beardsley was one of the inactive sisters, because she was a Blank; if she had been a Blanker, Mrs. Morris would have been as troubled as Mrs. Dean was about the new neighbor, though on a different principle.

As it was, she called on her after a while; but her time was so taken up with the Blanker church, her house was so filled and overrun with all the Blanker congregation, from the minister down to the sexton; she had so many weddings, and funerals, and societies to attend, that Mrs. Beardsley hardly saw her in her own house for the next year, though Mrs. Morris's call was promptly returned.

Next to Mrs. Roberts lived the Waters family; nice, kindly, plain young people; Mrs. Waters's sister being the third member of the family. The husband was a tinner, and it was in his shop, where she was buying a tea-kettle, that the new neighbor was introduced to them. They meant to call, they were members of the same church to which the Beardsleys belonged, and lived only two houses away; but they were so shy! It seemed to be a sort of agony to them to speak before a stranger; they blushed, and stammered, and looked every way but the right one. At last, after a year of waiting, they came one evening, but they never came again.

Up above her, for the street was on the side of a gentle declivity, Mrs. Beardsley had another neighbor, a carpenter's wife, Mrs. Green. She, too, seemed to be shy at first, but was attracted after a while by Justina's flowers and Tommy's merry face. She was childless herself, and her one passion was flowers, and after the ice was broken she came in often, sometimes with an apple for Tommy, sometimes with a rose for his mother. Mrs. Roberts had called Mrs. Beardsley proud and "stuck-up," but Mrs. Green did not find her so.

"She's real nice," was her unbiased verdict, as she walked home one night with the Waters family from prayer-meeting. "I did expect she'd be a little airy, seein' who her folks'was; but she ain't, not a mite. She's as pleasant as pie. I dunno when I've set so much by a new neighbor as I do by her. Mis' Dean's a leetle too high in the instep for me; and Mis' Morris, she don't care for nobody without they're a Blanker; and you can't take no solid comfort with Mis' Roberts, she's so partic'lar leest you shouldn't think so much of her as you'd ought to. But, my! Mis' Beardsley, she's just as easy as an old shoe. I wish't I hadn't stayed away so long, but you know, Malviny, I ain't no hand to make acquaintance with folks. I don't know as I should ever ha' knowed you if John hadn't been my nephew." Mrs. Waters gave a little laugh, but she did not say anything; she did not remember much about her own call on the new neighbor but her own painful shyness.

There was still another neighbor on the street,
old Miss Betsey Parker, the tailoress, who lived in
a small brown house next but one to that which
the Beardsleys occupied. She was a plain, unedu-
cated woman, having plenty of common sense and
a cheerful nature; no especial talent, or brightness,
or charm of aspect, but she was an honest and
humble Christian. Mrs. Dean sent her sewing,
when she had it; and Mrs. Morris found it very
handy to have a tailoress so close by when her two
big boys tore their clothes, especially as Miss
Betsey went to the Blanker church. Beside these
small sources of income she made shrouds from
the Dalton factory, and coffin· trimmings, the day
of tailoress work having gone by; and she owned
the little old house she lived in, which was set
about with cinnamon roses and lilacs, and had a
garden devoted chiefly to corn, beans and squashes,
though a great bunch of clove pinks and a cluster
of red peonies adorned its border. She was the
first neighbor whose acquaintance Mrs. Beardsley
made. While that weary woman was putting down
her parlor carpet, she looked up at the sound of a
kind voice, and saw a slat sunbonnet peering round
the edge of the door; deep in its gingham vault
Miss Betsey's cheerful face smiled at her. "I
thought mebbe I could help you someway. I live
next door but one, and if you want anything I've
got just send for it; matches, or salt, or an extry
hammer. I know how 'tis; folks always forget

somethin'. Mercy's sake! let me git hold of that stretcher! them poor little hands o' yourn ain't fit for such heavy work;" and suiting the action to the word she took Mrs. Beardsley's place, and the refractory carpet became docile at once, while poor Justina sat down on the floor and felt like crying from mere relief. "There! I wish 'twas the first instead o' the last. I live right up here in that small house with the lean-to, and if you want a thing I've got, to help ye, send right up. My name's Betsey Parker."

"Oh thank you. I was so tired!" was the rather incoherent answer; but the very grateful look out of Mrs. Beardsley's expressive eyes filled it out for Miss Betsey.

She had not stopped to consider her own position or her neighbor's, but came at once to see if she could help. And this was only the beginning; she brought many a fresh egg over to tempt Justina's delicate appetite, though her poultry was only three bantam hens. And again and again when her neighbor had a headache, she took Tommy home with her for the day, though she had sometimes to stay at home from church with him. She had no carriage like Mrs. Morris to give her neighbor a drive — as Mrs. Morris never did. She had no loaded fruit-trees like Mrs. Dean, who kept her pears and peaches for her own and the minister's family, exclusively; but her black-cap raspberries were more than shared with Mrs. Waters, as well as Mrs. Beardsley, and her currants were almost public property.

"I really hain't had enough for jell this year," she said apologetically to Mrs. Green, "and I do lot on jell, it's so good for the sick; but then, fresh currants is real refreshin' this hot weather, you know it's been master hot right along for a spell, and there ain't but a few has got as good currants as mine be."

At last Mrs. Beardsley fell ill of low fever; she was very lonely, for Fred had to be all day at his work, and the girl in the kitchen had her hands full with Tommy and the housework. The doctor's gig at the door notified the neighbors of the trouble, and after it had stopped there daily for a week, Mrs. Dean sent over her girl to inquire how Mrs. Beardsley was. Mrs. Morris met her husband in the street, and asked him the same question. Mrs. Roberts was not concerned about the matter. "Those upper-crust folks keep sending in to ask, I see; I haven't never called there, so I ain't wanted nor needed now as I know of."

But she did tell the doctor she was a good watcher, and would go if they couldn't get anybody else.

Mrs. Waters had a little baby, and could do nothing, yet she sent in a rosebud, the first from her one cherished bush, and Justina cried over it; she was so weak! Mrs. Green came over once or twice, and sent some custard; but she "wan't no use in sickness ; so dreadful nervous," her husband said.

Miss Betsey was out of town at first, but as soon as she came back not a day passed that she did not go over and cheer the sick woman with homely, earnest words of faith and hope and good-will. She went into the kitchen and made beef tea, she came up stairs and shook up her hot pillows, replenished the fire, combed out the tangled hair with the gentlest fingers, and kept Tommy with her in the intervals, as long as he could be coaxed to stay. When Mrs. Beardsley was getting better, the first day she could sit up, after Miss Betsey had made her comfortable with cushions and a footstool, the poor languid woman put her thin arms about the old lady's neck, and kissed her, and dropping her head on that sturdy shoulder burst into irrepressible sobs.

" Lawful sakes ! don't ye do so, child ! stop right off. Why, you'll be all tuckered out when he gets home, ef you do so. Now, stop right off !"

" I can't help it," sobbed Tina ; " you're so good, Miss Betsey ; you're a real angel !"

"The mortal ! You must be out o' your mind, child. Who ever saw an angel with yaller-gray hair and not but six teeth to show for't ?" laughed the good old soul. "You stop cryin' and talkin' about angels, and swaller your beef tea, or the doctor'll be scoldin' of ye, for certain sure."

When Mrs. Beardsley was well enough for

change of air, she went into Dalton to see her sister, who had but just come back from Europe, and was naturally eager to hear all about Tina's surroundings.

"And have you got any neighbors, dear?" she asked, after many other questions.

"One," said Justina, smiling.

The question still remains to be answered:

"Who was Mrs. Beardsley's neighbor?"

JESUS — FIRST AND LAST.

EVERYTHING in **Jesus Christ** astonishes me. So said Napoleon Bonaparte at St. Helena; and then he added: " The birth of Jesus, the story of His life, the profoundness of His doctrines which overturn all difficulties, His empire, His progress through all centuries, all this is to me a prodigy! It is great with a greatness that crushes me." What a contrast was there to Napoleon between the empire of the Cross and his own imperial image of " iron and clay," which had been set up at the cost of a million of lives, and which had been shattered to pieces by the moral indignation of Europe!

If Jesus Christ appeared wonderful to the fallen giant at St. Helena even when glanced at occasionally, how much more wonderful is He to those of us who study Him with both the head and the heart. He not only "astonishes" us; He enchants and captivates. Whenever we open our Bibles we see Jesus; just as whenever we look up at Chamouny we see Mont Blanc. In the earlier part of the Old Testament we descry the august form of the Messiah somewhat enveloped by mists — like

Mont Blanc at early dawn — but as we go on farther into the ancient word, the mists steadily move off, until in the New Testament we see none but Jesus only, in His unclouded glory. He is the Alpha and the Omega of the whole Bible, the beginning and the end, the first and the last. In Genesis He appears as the "seed of the woman." The smoke of Abel's altar points towards Him. Old dying Jacob catches a glimpse of Him as the advancing "Shiloh" from his couch of death. The blood that stains the Jewish lintels on the night of the exodus, is but a type of that Lamb of God who taketh away the sins of the world! Moses and the prophets all testify of Jesus. Just as the rich sonorous blast of an Alpine horn on the Wengern is echoed back from the peak of the Jungfrau, so every verse of the fifty-third chapter of Isaiah is echoed in the New Testament story of Jesus. In short, the Bible is so full of Christ that He is its Alpha and Omega ; His name is the key to unlock the Old Testament, and the crown to glorify the New.

The man who loves his Bible best, loves Jesus above every other. He is often ready to cry out with the impassioned fervor of Rutherford : "Woe upon all love but the love of Christ! A hunger forevermore be upon all heaven but Christ ; a shame forevermore be upon all but Christ's glory! I cry death be upon all manner of life but the life of Christ! I would not exchange one smile of His

lovely face for kingdoms. He is a Rose that beau-
tifieth all the Upper Garden of God — a leaf of
that rose of God for smell is worth a world.
Oh! His sweetness, His weight, His overpassing
beauty!" In such rapturous expressions did one
of Christ's martyrs set forth his heart-loyalty to
the Saviour in whom his soul delighted. The language seems extravagant and **Oriental** to those who
have never tasted of the love of Jesus, or rested on
His bosom in hours of sore trial.

If the Bible be so full of Christ, and the experiences of the best and holiest Christians have
exuded with Christ like honey from the pressed
honeycomb; then our preaching ought to be full of
Christ Jesus also. That is the best sermon which
presents the Saviour of sinners the most clearly,
prominently and powerfully to a congregation of
sinners. That is the most strengthening and comforting discourse for God's people which brings
them closest to His everlasting arms. When a
minister has been holding up before his auditors
the exceeding sinfulness of sin, and the sure retri-
butions of the "wrath to come," oh! how his soul
rejoices to lift up before them that crucified Jesus
whose blood cleanseth from all sin. It would be
the refinement of cruelty to preach the depravity
and hell-deservings of the human heart, if we could
not follow with the swift, sure remedy for all this
wretched guilt in Jesus Christ, the Redeemer.

There is a *system* of salvation in the inspired

Word — yes! and a system of heaven-inspired theology, too, that runs through the Scriptures as a system of physical laws runs through the sunlight and the stellar universe. But it is not the system that saves the sinner, or comforts the saint. It is Christ — the living, personal Saviour — the center and subject of the system, but as much greater than the system as the sun is greater than the manual of astronomy which a schoolboy studies. When your limb is beginning to mortify, you don't want a treatise on surgery ; you want the skillful surgeon. What our people need to know is to know who can cleanse away their guilt, who can secure their pardon, who can deliver them from the power of the devil, who can relieve their distresses, who can bear their burdens, who can endue them with strength to conquer, and who can save their immortal souls. They want a pattern to live by. They want a guide. They want a Friend ever near to show them through life's dark places, and to help them in its places of danger. Simply for ethical purposes, there is no preaching so instructive and effective as the clear presentation of Christ Jesus as our perfect model. Church-members never steal trust-funds, never lie, never default, when they have their eye upon their Divine Master, and are striving to walk as they have him for an ensample. Our young converts never get into ball-rooms, or gambling-parties, or impure resorts, or revelings, while they are trying to please Jesus. A system, or a church-covenant, don't affect the conscience like a *look from a personal divine Saviour;* especially where loyalty to that Saviour is accompanied by His gracious omnipotent help to keep us in the straight path. For one, I am never uneasy about those members of my flock who make Christ their Alpha and their Omega. They never make me blush for them, or give me a wakeful hour.

I am also fully persuaded that the most effectual antidote to the current skepticism of the times is to present the incarnate Son of God continually. *Christ is the only cure for infidelity !* Young brother in the ministry! cut that truth as with the pen of a diamond on your heart, and on your work! No skeptic can out-general you, or worst you, on that ground. If you can get him there, and keep him there, the Cross may conquer him.

Guido's great painting of the " Aurora," on the frescoed ceilings of the Roman palace, is hard to look at; but when reflected in a mirror on the floor, it can be easily studied for hours. So Jesus reflects GOD to us. Beholding as in a mirror, with open face, this glory of the infinite God, we may be changed into a likeness to that image, from glory to glory, as by the Spirit of the Lord. So let us all study Jesus, and trust Jesus, and obey Jesus, that we may resemble Him more and more till we go up to " see Him as He is !"

ONLY A STEP-MOTHER.

HE child is never dressed in any kind of style. She always looks as if the odds and ends of everybody's clothes had been sewed together to cover her up. Has she any mother ?

This question was asked by a lady standing before a long mirror while her maid was looping up and tying back her drapery, preparatory for a great public reception or ball.

" Only a step-mother," replied the waiting friend, as she turned her hand in the light to catch the flash of her diamonds. " Only a step-mother ; and she, poor young thing, must have a doleful time of it as well as the children. She actually wears the same cloak she had when she was married three years ago. But it is nobody's fault but her own; for she must have known how much of his property Mr. Cornell had lost, and what a tribe of youngsters he had to feed and clothe. It does seem a shame for her to have had such a downfall, a girl of such taste and such sweetness of temper. I remember how we all admired and perhaps envied her tiny gold watch and emerald ring at school. Poor girl ! She was very beautiful."

"I don't pity her at all!" cried the lady at the glass, with much emphasis. "She must have had a low taste—not shown out in her girlhood—or she would never have thrown away her beauty, and the position it promised her, on a widower in a two-story house with three children and one servant. I don't care a straw for your old schoolmate, though I do pity the children she dresses out of her rag-bag, maybe with their dead mother's clothes! I only wish that pretty little Kitty wouldn't cleave to my Bess as she does. I'm so afraid strangers will think she is one of my children!"

The last rose was now fixed in the folds of the dress, the last glove buttoned, and the last admiring glance cast into the mirror; and then the woman who pitied the child with "only a step-mother," left her own baby sleeping in the care of an irresponsible Irish nurse, who might, and probably would, join the "gang" in the kitchen as soon as the carriage rolled away. Two older children called from their cribs in the next room: "Don't stay long, mamma; Bridget is so cross when you're gone."

And the mother, bent on pleasure, called back with a wink at her friend: "No, dears; mamma will be back before daylight!"

And then these two "silken wonders" shone and sparkled in the dance as if they had never had a sorrow or a care, when in reality their laces and jewels covered aching and disappointed hearts.

The brown-stone house, with story piled on story,

where the little children lay worrying and fretting
for their "own mother;" with all the pictures, and
statuary, and drapery, and jewels it contained,
were the price of blood.   Its owner had heaped up
gold on the ruin of a thousand homes and ten
thousand broken hearts. Of course he was "a
respectable man in the community, and never sold
a *single* glass of liquor in his life;" but he had
sold barrels and hogsheads and pipes and tierces
enough to make millions of " single glasses," each
one of which, with the ruin it had wrought, was set
down to his account against the great day of reck-
oning!

These high crimes against God and man had
never cost the gay wife a tear nor an hour's sleep.
But something else had! She was quite willing
other homes should be laid in ashes, but she wanted
her own kept bright; quite willing other wives
should lose the love and the tender care of their
husbands, but she wanted her husband to have no
charm beyond his own home and his own family.

But no man can spend his days defiling and ruin-
ing others, without being himself defiled and
ruined.   The business of a man's life tells on his
character for good or evil.   Fast horses, clubs, the
gaming table and the wine cup, were telling rapidly
on him.   He spent little time at home, although
his pride in his fine house, stylish wife and pretty
children, induced him to shower money, in any
amount, upon them.   While this gratified his wife,

his neglect chagrined, mortified, **and** perhaps **wounded her ;** and **drove her out** into the follies of the **world in search of the** peace and **joy a good true wife and mother** finds chiefly at **home.**

A very different life was led by the woman who was " only a step-mother," and who lived, as the other thought, contemptibly, " in a two-story house, with three children **and** one servant."

Misfortune has not **the** power to wreck all homes ; many are built above its reach, and lie secure from the winds and tempests of earth, as if in the hollow of God's **hand, where even** that **severing** of bonds **which must come alike to all, is but the signal for a blessed and permanent reunion.**

One of these " homes **of the blessed" was that presided over by this " step-mother."** She had not **married blindly, nor in haste ; she knew well** what she **was** doing, **and for whom she** was **to** labor, when she took up **the work a** sainted woman had laid down in **strong hope and earnest trust** in God. She knew **the man she** loved, and in whom her **heart trusted, had met** with business reverses, and **that as an honest man he must** greatly reduce **his style of living ; she knew also** that his sweet, **moth-erless children** would **bring on her labor and cares unknown before ; but she counted the cost, took up her life's** work, and **had matured into a bright,** strong **and brave woman.** By her rare tact and management she had **encouraged her** husband **to** regain step by step **the footing he** had lost, and

inspired him with a belief that as he had retained
his honor and the good opinion of all, even of those
who had lost money through him, he might yet be
the counselor and helper of many in financial
troubles.

She relieved him of every home care, made his
children as happy as they had ever been, and
reduced his domestic expenses to a low figure,
compared with those incurred by his housekeeper
before her coming. She kept his heart true to her
and his home, making that the brightest and sun-
niest spot on earth to him.

She taught his children — her children she called
them — the sweet lessons of their own mother,
whose image she strove to keep fresh in their
minds, and before whose picture in the parlor she
encouraged them to keep, always, a little vase of
fresh flowers; and impressed on them the truth
that, if they followed her pure example, they would
surely meet her by and by in the beautiful home
where she was waiting for them.

This lovely woman gave the best years of her life
to the work she had taken at the hands of God;
and although she saw nothing of the world of
fashion, she was a truly happy woman. Her home
was her kingdom, her reward was present and very
great; and the love of these children was a crown
to her.

As the years wore on, great success crowned her
husband's efforts. He stood again, while yet in

middle life, in his former place in business circles; and his generosity prompted him, as far as he could do so honorably, to surround his family with all the real refinements of life which they were so well able to appreciate and enjoy. This step-mother had enjoyed life as it went by, even amid some cares and privations; and she never saw the day that she envied any man's wife her costly home, rich wardrobe or rare jewels. And now that she had all that heart could desire, she shared her blessings with others, and so was herself doubly blessed.

If there is work in this world worthy of angel's hands, it is hers who takes up the gentle words and tireless ministrations of a sainted mother, and makes her bereaved children happy!

If there is a woman on earth who deserves the sympathy and love of other women, it is she who is thus filling up another's measure of love to the motherless. If the redeemed in glory can follow with purified vision the beloved of earth in all their ways — and shall any one dare to say they cannot? — what benedictions must be hourly falling on the heads of those of whom the heartless may say: "They are only step-mothers."

While this lovely woman's abundant brown hair was still untouched by time, the home where she was ridiculed, "pitied," was no more a home! The last diamonds had sparkled there, and the last roses been twined in the rich garments of its heartless mistress.

The serpent in the wine cup had struck at the heart of the husband and father with his poisoned fangs; and although he had never sold "a single glass of liquor," he had drank thousands of them, to his ruin!

He was now alienated from his wife, and from his children, none of whom had skill or faculty to earn their living, and so were scattered, in miserable dependence, among half a dozen relatives.

"Little Kitty" and "Bess" had kept their baby friendship unbroken, and now the sweet unfortunate was invited to pass a year with the young girl who had "only a step-mother," in the full hope that her accomplishments might be so directed as to become a source of independence to herself, and, perhaps, to her disheartened mother and the little children.

And she is learning now, in that happy home, that life is something more than a holiday, and that the world is more than a mere playground.

LESSONS LEARNED BY SICKNESS.

VERY one hears of the humiliations of sickness. There are enough of those. For a grown man, a man well on in years, who had begun to think he had some rights for others to respect, to be treated like a baby — with no will worth speaking of ; his food, drink, medicine, rest, such, and given at such times as suit other people's notions ; to be laid on the right side or the left, on the spine or the nose, as his keepers choose, does not tend to greaten his self-esteem unduly. Then, for long days and nights to be so heavily poulticed as to one side of the head that, when lifted, it wobbles like that of one of Nast's rag-babies, does not largely swell one's pride. No more does a string of blisters, to make room for which venerable locks have been closely shorn. And when, beside these, comes along a Swedish pumping firm, the "Leech Brothers," and after careful survey sink several wells back of the ear and down the neck, robbing one of his very life-blood, that one thing which he called his own, he finds of how little account he really is. Thenceforth he not only sees how it is that the world can go on as well without as with him, but he becomes very willing it should.

Yet to this there is an offset. This sick old infant sees that, after all, entire household arrangements are shaped to meet his single needs. The tenderest care of the best beloved, aided by old friends, is not too precious to be lavished on him day and night, through long, restless, wearing weeks. The wisest physicians give him their time, their skill, their careful study, and the best results of their long experience. Thoughtful friends send in costly delicacies — flowers, perfumes, rare fruits, preserves and jellies. Daily calls from neighbors, letters of inquiry and sympathy from many in all parts of the land whom the good love to honor — these and many like things help to hold the balance even, show what a warm place the sick man has in many true hearts, and keep him from giving up life in utter disgust.

Of great worth is that new view the sick man gets of the closeness and delicacy of the link between the body and the mind ; the thinness of the line between sound and unsound mental states and acts. What more real (to himself) than a sick man's dreams and fancies, that so quickly vanish with the sunrise ? What speeches he makes ; what sermons he preaches ; what new grand inventions are those of his half-waking, half-sleeping night hours ; what plans for the profit of himself and others, to be surely executed to-morrow, but which to-morrow he laughs at ! He must be a hard man in whom such experience does not waken fresh thankfulness to the divine love that carries mind and body safely through years of toil, care, exposure ; forces from without and within that might so easily sway the mind from the pivot of sanity, and leave it to shoot off into fatal wreck.

It is worth going through such a time of weakness and pain to get the "realizing sense" it gives of many truths which one knew all about before : the value of tried friendship ; the true use of time, talents, money ; the full meaning and blessedness of our Father's best earthly gifts — Christian marriage and home ; the strong comfort of a settled definite religious faith ; the aspect that death wears when looked at as a near reality, and no longer as a far-off shadow. Everybody knows that a sick bed is no place to prepare for death. He who has been there not only knows, but believes it. And he will grudge no pain or fear that has tested the clearness of his trust in the Gospel, and the strength of his hold on the Saviour it reveals — faith and trust which it is one thing to profess in the sunlight, and quite another to anchor the soul upon in darkness and storm.

The man has not been very sick who doubts, as so many try to doubt, that there is to be a final judgment. "What folly," some say, "to believe that God can, if He would, keep a true record of all one's earthly life, and bring him to account for it." But when, face to face with death, one has seen trooping back not only the sins of his whole life, but his foibles, and even little boyish slips in matters of mere etiquette, forgotten long ago, he does not have to be told that no formal record from without will be needed; on each soul its life's story is branded; each conscience will bring along its own account.

Nor will such a one doubt that God can and should punish unrepented sin. Life's near-coming end gives a new hue and meaning to its purpose, opportunities, responsibilities; weighs anew its values; sounds with new line and plummet the guilt of him who wastes or abuses it. And when, in visions of the night, the Almighty causes to rise before a soul that has so measured life, those living wheels of his power and law that Ezekiel saw, "so high that they were dreadful," he will thenceforth hide his face, and never more presume to "contend with Him that is mightier than he."

But with brighter visions the morning sun, emblem of the Sun of Righteousness, irradiates the tears of the penitent. From the horizon to the zenith rise those gates of the city through which the pardoned enter. As he gazes the solid pearl seems to change to living beings, angels and seraphs, whose moving wings, glowing with tints of opal, sapphire, emerald and amethyst, beckon him onward. At his approach the living portals roll back. Far within, on a great white throne, sits

One on whose face he dares not look. Along the golden streets a blessed company hasten to meet the new comer. Familiar faces smile upon him, and warm hands of parents, sisters, spiritual children, brethren in the Lord's service, welcome him to the Father's house. The circle opens, and over the shining pavement comes running with outspread arms a fair-haired child, with the same joyous laugh and greeting as of old. In the rapture of that meeting the dream is broken. It is hard to come back from that vision of sinless joy and rest to this world of work and trial and sin. But henceforth it can hardly be the same world it has been. Mayhap yet one more will be able to sing, "It is good for me that I have been afflicted, that I might learn thy precepts."

HIRAM LYNDE'S EXPERIMENT.

"Full many a shaft at random sent,
Finds mark the archer little meant."

F Hiram Lynde had been an Irishman, or
an African, he would have been amply satisfied with his position as gardener and
hostler for Mark Harrington, Esq., which yielded
him good wages. But he was a stanch, northern
Vermonter, who found it hard to realize there is a
wide social distinction between the employer and
employé in the suburbs of New York. To be considered an upper servant, and to be forced to eat
in the kitchen with Bridget Malone and Ann
McCarty, chafed his pride terribly.

Every Sunday Hiram harnessed a pair of superb
black horses into a costly, soft-cushioned carriage,
and drove the Harrington family to church. While
they were worshiping within, he waited outside,
or rode slowly around the streets to pass away the
time, but was always promptly back, when the congregation dispersed, to take them home.

Month after month went by. Bitter feelings, in
the meantime, had gained mastery in Hiram

Lynde's heart, and angry mutterings were often on his lips, which he found hard to suppress.

One fine morning he drove with the Harringtons to church as usual. As they slowly ascended the steps, and disappeared within the sanctuary, a strange light shone in his eyes, and, shaking his hand fiercely after them, he exclaimed :

"Proud hypocrites ! There they go to worship God, and advertise their fine fortune, through their velvets, silks and laces. They put money into the contribution-box for the poor with their jeweled hands ; but nary a farthing do they care for the souls of one of them. Nearly a year I've brought them regularly to church, but nobody has said a word about my going *in*. If preaching is good for them, why isn't it for *me*, too ? Ah, I'll try an experiment. I'll bring their fashionable religion out into a strong light, or prove it all a sham. Ha ! ha ! yes, I will."

Four days passed. A purpose had ripened in Hiram's breast, and he longed to put it into execution.

One morning as he was weeding in Mr. Harrington's garden, he saw Joe Phelps leaning against the gate.

"Holloa, Joe ! come here," he called pleasantly.

Joe skipped up the gravel walk to his side. His mother was a hard-toiling widow, who earned a scanty livelihood for herself and six children by washing. Joe's clothes were so worn that great patches covered his knees and elbows, and only great skill in mending and darning held them together. Hiram surveyed him closely.

"Pretty poor clothes you wear; hardly fit for a pauper," he remarked sneeringly.

"They are the best I have," replied Joe, the hot blood mounting to his face from wounded pride.

"Want a chance to earn a new suit in an easy way, in one hour?" asked Hiram.

"Yes, indeed," answered Joe, joyfully.

"Joe, I'll make you a fair, square offer. Next Sunday morning, if you'll wear these same old clothes, and be barefooted just as you are now, and go into church just after the Harringtons get in, and take a seat in their pew with them — it's number 105 — I'll give you the best suit of summer clothes in Darrow's store."

"Oh, you are foolin'," laughed Joe.

"Never was more serious in my life," said Hiram earnestly. "I want to mortify these purse-proud Christians. I want to see how these big feeling people will act, to be in a row with a poor boy, half-covered with patches and darns."

"Oh, I don't want to go into their pew," said Joe quickly. "'Tisn't using them well; it's mean."

"As you please," replied Hiram indifferently. "There's plenty of other boys who'd jump at my offer."

Joe reflected a moment. "Yes, I'll do it," he said decidedly. "Mother would have to do a great deal of washing to get me a summer suit. I'll do it to save her ; but I hate to awfully."

When Sunday came, Joe waited till he saw the elegant carriage of Mark Harrington go by, and then followed hard after it. He reached the church just after the family had entered it. Hiram was holding the horses in front of the steps. Giving the reins to a friend standing by, he and Joseph made their way through the vestibule, up the stairs to the inner door. Here Hiram waited, and watched, with a chuckling heart, the boy as he timorously went through the broad aisle till he came to pew number 105. Mr. Harrington was sitting at the foot, and Joe slipped in by him, and sat down between him and his daughter Helen, while the faces of both showed great surprise.

" That was capitally done," thought Hiram exultingly. " Joe is a trump anywhere. Now the rich and poor sit side by side, and in God's eyes one is no better than the other."

On their way home, the odd incident of Joseph Phelps's sitting uninvited in their pew was glibly discussed by the Harringtons.

" Poor boy," said Miss Helen, pityingly, "it is plain his starved soul is reaching out for something higher. We must encourage and help him."

" But it was so funny to see him pop down by you. I thought I should laugh outright," said Miss Fannie.

Hiram listened in astonishment. No word of

indignation or mortification came from the lips
of these he had called fashionable Christians. His
plan to humble their pride had failed.

On Monday, Joseph came around to receive the
promised remuneration for his service. Hiram was
true to his word, and gave him a good summer suit
of clothes, which made him very happy. Towards
evening Joseph Phelps received a notice, through
Bridget Malone, the cook, that her master, Mark
Harrington, wished to see him.

He entered that gentleman's presence tremblingly. He had committed a grave offense by
taking a seat beside him uninvited, and he was in
quivering expectation of being accused of it.

"Joseph, did you enjoy hearing Mr. Catlin preach
yesterday?" asked Mr. Harrington with an amused
smile.

"No—yes—I guess I did—I don't know, sir,"
was the stammering reply, with wild, frightened
eyes, and a face spotted like an adder. A low
giggle came from Miss Fannie, who was sitting in
the bay window with Miss Helen. "Do you want
to keep on going to church?" asked Mr. Harrington, kindly and encouragingly.

"Yes, sir."

"Then you shall. I'll give you an order to take
to Mr. Darrow, and you may select such a suit of
clothes as you need, and I'll pay for them." A
joyful light bounded into Joseph's eyes.

"Father," said Miss Helen, "he'll need a hat,

and boots, stockings and handkerchief. Let me get him these," and turning to Joseph she inquired: "How would you like to go into Mr. Crawford's class of boys in the Sunday school?"

"Oh, very much, ma'am," in a choking voice.

"I'll ask him to receive you."

"I own a pew, number forty, in the gallery," said Mr. Harrington. "You can have a seat there. You are a good boy. All you need is a chance to rise in the world, Joseph."

"Thank you, thank you, sir. Thank you, Miss Harrington. I shall never forget your kindness; never, *never*, NEVER;" and with gratitude shining in his eyes he left the house.

Twenty-four hours after, Joseph appeared before Hiram Lynde dressed in his best.

"Do I look like a pauper now?" he questioned proudly.

"No; you look like a gentleman's son. Where did you get all those new clothes?"

"Mr. Harrington gave me this suit; and Miss Helen gave me my hat, stockings and boots; and I'm going to keep on going to church, and am going into the Sunday school."

"By jingo; this beats all creation!" exclaimed the amazed Hiram.

"I'm in luck," went on Joseph gayly. "You gave me a suit of clothes for sitting in Mr. Harrington's pew, and they've given me another. It was a tip-top bargain you made with me."

12

"It's cost me half a month's wages;" responded Hiram. "Well, they've done handsomely by you; that's a fact. They never took no more notice of me than if I'd been a worm. I thought their religion was all a sham. Well, my experiment didn't humble them, after all; it just set 'em up higher."

This conversation had a listener least expected.

Miss Helen was standing behind a spruce tree, and every word came straight to her ears. She went into the house and faithfully reported them. "'Twas a trick of Hiram's," she said. "He wanted to prove our profession. We haven't been kind and considerate enough of him. He is a good man, and we ought to treat him differently — just as if we were in his place, and he in ours."

Hiram Lynde's experiment proved highly beneficial in three ways. He learned by it that "fashionable Christians" even, who wear velvet, silks, and jewels, have often noble hearts which beat in helpful sympathy for the needy. It was the means of introducing Joseph Phelps to Mr. Harrington and his family, and they ever after took a deep interest in his welfare. Finally, it revealed to the Harringtons the duty of being more considerate towards those serving them, and the lesson was never forgotten.

On sped the years, bringing many changes. Hiram Lynde is a respected, useful man. By carefully saving his earnings, and the loan of a few hundred dollars from Mr. Harrington, he has been able to purchase a fine little farm, which made him very happy.

Joseph Phelps is a successful merchant. He is always loyal to the right, a light in his church and a blessing wherever he goes.

NEVER AND NO MORE.

NOT death himself
Hath hands so flinty, and so freezing cold,
As hath this never. Over what *was* ours
Death leaves with most of us a dim perhaps
That floats through silence, undefined in form,
Tormenting Fancy, not destroying Hope.
No More! Intense is this in awfulness;
But its dread fiat not to be revoked —
That death, or circumstance, that living death,
Must put an endless end to all most dear —
Is far less terrible than Never's is,
Because the very *more* implies the *once*.
Never is merciless beyond compare,
Because the precious once dies in his clutch,
That once which makes the always of great souls.
Somewhere in every heart the Never strikes,
Dealing a death-blow to some begging wish;
If for an object that is loved as life,
It is as though importunate desire
Were the undying soul of dying Hope
Whose body this relentless Never kills,
Leaving its spirit in eternal thirst,

MIRACLES.

———

T is one of the curious phases of modern opinion, that men who are foremost in their demand for actual facts, and in their defense of the Baconian method which requires that all prejudices be removed, and the actual facts of observation be accepted, whatever they may be, should also, when the fact of a miracle is in question, be equally forward to deny it, because a certain theory of nature which they have come to entertain makes a miracle impossible. But such a theory not only contradicts the true method of scientific inquiry, but it contradicts itself, as can be seen by any one whose eyes are clear. For, to say that a miracle is impossible because contrary to the facts of my experience, is absurd, unless the facts of my experience embrace all the possible facts of any experience, to claim which would be a greater absurdity still.

Again, to say that no such fact as a miracle can be, because certain other facts, which I have learned from this source and that, and which I am pleased to call "the order of nature," forbids it, leads one to ask for a more precise designation of this order of nature, and for the proof that it actually exists. This proof must either rest within the field of our experience, that is, it must be a proof to which our experience actually testifies, or one respecting which our experience has no witness whatever. But our experience, at the farthest, only testifies to that which is, and never reaches to that which can be. If my experience contain nothing miraculous, I may of course deny the existence of a miracle so far as my experience reaches, and if my judgments rest only on what I have experienced, that is, if they be only inferences from what I actually see, I am not entitled to make any affirmations respecting what lies beyond ; and that a miracle has not taken place in another experience than my own, is quite out of my province to say. The moment I make such a sweeping assertion as to affirm or deny anything universal, I must leave the ground of my experience, which is necessarily partial and limited, and take my stand on a basis back of experience and reaching beyond it. But such a groundwork lies also back of nature, and inevitably leads the thought into the living presence of the supernatural.

Our natural science is fond of its generalizations, but no generalization is possible without the supernatural. It is an unmeaning babble to talk of comprehensive laws, unless there be a comprehending reason and will, whose ideas and plans these laws express. The current notion in some quarters, that we can gain, or have perchance got, such universal conclusions that nature can be shut in upon itself and God shut out, is exactly the absurdity of supposing that we see when we have closed our eyes, and turned the very light of all our seeing into darkness. Every process of the human mind bears witness to the Divine Mind. Every thought we can have of nature, when profoundly questioned is seen to rest upon the knowledge, undoubting and universal, that nature has its living author, its spiritual creator. But cannot He who has made nature also unmake it if He will, or order in it whatever changes He may please? And if men who did not like to retain God in their thoughts, professing themselves to be wise, became fools, because that when they knew God they glorified Him not as God, neither were thankful, but became vain in their imaginations, and their foolish hearts were darkened; what is to hinder Him, if His love impels it, from making such changes in nature as shall more conspicuously manifest Himself, and more gloriously carry forward the eternal purpose for which He hath created all things by Jesus Christ?

Such changes are miracles. They are not contradictions to nature, but they are the carrying of nature upward to a higher plane, and onward to grander results than nature, in its unhindered action, alone could reach. They are not to be considered as violations of the order of nature; rather are they the cropping out in nature of the higher

order of the supernatural, without which the so-
called order of nature would be but an empty
chaos; they are rifts in the clouds of the earth's
atmosphere, through which the glories of the
heavens, which make the clouds resplendent, and
the earth radiant, can shine. They are not the new
development of some old force which had been in
nature from the beginning, but they are a new creation by which new forces, henceforth to work in
harmony with the old, are added to these. Surely
such changes are possible for God to make.
Surely, He who hath created once, can do it also
again. Surely, if the inspiration of genius may
sometimes light up the human face with a glow
which shows the glory of the soul beyond all ordinary thoughts; if the light of love may sometimes
lend a luster to the eye through which there shines
a look of beauty before unknown — much more
may the aspect of the things which are made, in
which the eternal Power and Godhead of their
Maker have from the creation of the world been
clearly seen, take on some altogether new expression, and become radiant with a glory all undiscov-
ered before; when He would reveal through them
also His forgiving and renewing love. Surely all
this is possible, and miracles, instead of being irra-
tional and inconceivable, are the very beauty of
reason, and the very light of our thoughts respecting nature, when they are correctly apprehended.
Creation itself is a miracle. The most recent

science, in the profound mathematical demonstrations of Clausius respecting the mechanical theory of heat, has shown, on scientific grounds alone, the need of some higher power than nature, in order to its origination, and therefore miracles cannot be impossible at any stage of nature's continuance.

The only proper attitude towards this question, and the only truly scientific method, is to inquire whether such occurrences have actually taken place — an inquiry whose answer is only to be gained through a careful sifting of the evidence which declares them. If we find wonders reported which turn out to be no miracles, but only delusions of witchcraft and magic, these no more militate against the reality of miracles, than does an abundance of counterfeits against the reality of genuine coin. If we find some miracles reported for which the evidence fails, this no more precludes our finding others of undoubted verity, than do false statements in other matters prevent us from learning anything true. Let the quality of the reported miracle and its evidence be sifted to the utmost, and while we reject nothing from preconceived skepticism, let nothing be taken in credulous superstition. Let the eye be open and clear, and the heart receptive and responsive only to the truth, and if miracles are proved by sufficient testimony to have taken place, the wise man will accept them, and follow their conclusions, whatever these may be.

A FUNERAL SCENE.

HEY said she was dead. We knew she had been dying the last twenty-four hours; but she had always looked such a picture of health and activity, that in this case death seemed almost impossible. Not yet fifty years old, she was known probably to more people in, and out of town, than any other of her sex among us. Refinement and elegance characterized her home, and she was the center of its attractions. Six children, some already with families of their own, called her mother; and one of them spoke the feeling of others in similar circumstances in the remark that when she died it seemed as though everything must stop; and yet the world moved on all the same.

Four months she had suffered, though with little foreshadowing of a fatal result till within a few weeks. But she had grown worse and worse, and now the end had come. At first she had drawn back, instinctively; but soon she came to feel that God's way was right. Then letting go her hold upon earth, and with a personal faith in Christ as her Saviour, she calmly set her face heavenward.

Life certainly had attractions for her, if for anybody; and no one, perhaps, knows how hard she
found it to give them up. But at length she did
this, and did it cheerfully; thus verifying the saying of the apostle: "I can do all things through
Christ which strengtheneth me."

The spacious house was thronged at the funeral
service. The Ladies' Benevolent Society, the Sabbath school, the choir, and various other social
assemblies, had often gathered in that hospitable
home; but never before such a meeting as this.
Many came from out of town, and from the various
walks in life, public and private; for the sympathy
and esteem of all could center upon this stricken
household.

The family remained up stairs. The casket,
with an ample background of flowers, was placed
in the bay window, two of the pall-bearers standing
at its head and two at its foot. A lyre, crosses,
beautiful wreaths, a sickle, and various other
emblems, made up the floral tribute, which was all
that taste and love could suggest. First came the
Scripture reading; then an address from a former
pastor and life-long neighbor, who had written
out his words, not daring to trust his emotions.
Another pastor and friend of the family followed
with remarks and prayer. The chanting of the
twenty-third psalm and an appropriate song by a
quartette were also in the service; and, in closing,
the assembly joined in one verse of the hymn:
"Nearer, my God, to Thee."

The congregation was requested to retire after viewing the remains. The family then came down and were alone with their dead; and who can think of such a scene and such a parting without a feeling of solemnity and awe? It is a mystery how the custom of looking for the last time upon the faces of our beloved dead in the presence of a throng, either at home or at the church, can have prevailed so long here in New England.

The family passed quietly out to their carriages, the pall-bearers deposited the remains tenderly in the hearse at the door, and the procession moved on to the city of the dead. At the grave the voice of prayer was again raised, and the benediction pronounced, followed by a suppressed "Amen" from the sorrowing group. Then was addressed to the pall-bearers, with trembling voice, the charge: " I commit to you, my friends, these precious remains, to see that they are properly buried;" and the mourning circle slowly reëntered their carriages. The casket was placed in its box and lowered to its last resting-place. The bearers remained to see the grave filled and to arrange the flowers, which covered it to the full; and then with the remark: " We can do nothing more," they also withdrew, leaving the dead in the loneliness of the narrow house.

This husband and wife had grown up in one another's affections almost from childhood. The family had been a model of unity and the domestic joys, and I can hardly imagine an instance where family ties are stronger, and where such an inroad upon the home circle would be a keener and more terrible bereavement; and yet this grief seemed to be kept well under control. It certainly did not show itself in any tumultuous way, but was calm and subdued, though with most unmistakable indications of such a depth and burden of sorrow as the heart feels only seldom in a lifetime.

Skeptics may ask their troublesome questions in regard to the resurrection, as to *what* shall rise, and how it can be that we are to see the same body; but those who are firmly anchored in the truths of God's word, while they may not be able to answer in detail all these cavils, will, nevertheless, with unshaken confidence, believe what God has revealed, and see no occasion whatever for a shadow of doubt that the being who can create a world can also recreate man in another sphere of life. Paul has told us as clearly as any of the modern skeptics, that it will not be that body which is here laid away in the grave; and all we need now to know is that the identity is in some way to be preserved, and that somehow the same principle of life, in the same person, is to come forth in a new form beyond the grave.

THE RULING FASHION IN DEATH.

"'My young master in London is dead!' said Obadiah. A green satin night-gown of my mother's, which had been twice scoured, was the first idea which Obadiah's exclamation brought into Susannah's head." — *Sterne.*

WHAT woman, in any position or rank of social life, rich or poor, mistress or maid, has not felt Susannah's "first idea" irresistibly pressing upon her wounded spirit in the first moments of her grief for a loved one just gone? What woman, weeping in silence under the shadow of this great affliction, has not felt it deepened and blackened by the vision of sable millinery, which a pagan fashion prescribes as a public dress for her sorrow? Pagan fashion? No; it cannot be charged to a heathen lineage or custom. It is the outcome of our Christian civilization in these latter days of elegant shows and costly pretensions.

Is there enough of working vitality in the Christian life of this boastful generation to lift these heavy and grievous burdens from the house of God and the house of the dead? See how they grow upon both, making it more and more costly for a humble Christian to live and to die. Already the church and the cemetery have become the two great rival centers of modern fashion, and the undertaker's and milliner's shops well stocked feeders for both. The church of today is the most attractive center of fashion. It is filled, unlike the opera or theater, with a permanent, almost unchanging congregation of men, women and children, mostly known to each other in week-day life, and more susceptible of the desire and tendency to imitate, emulate, and even to provoke each other to envy in matters of dress and fashion, than is the case with the varying and incidental company assembled at a theatrical performance or place of general amusement. Indeed, it may be said within the truth, that all the varying styles of dress for men, women and children have more reference to the church as their show-room than to all other places and persons put together.

Thus, religious worship in the house of God has become one of the most highly taxed luxuries in every one of our growing and populous towns. Even our smart little villages are ambitious to follow city models, and do not think of building a church under the cost of $50,000 or $60,000. Then, probably owing half that amount for it at its opening, they must have a minister of as nearly city grade and salary as possible, whose talent, genius, and ardent devotion shall fill the house

with the most well-to-do of the village, who can pay
as well as appreciate such sermons and services.
Then the choir must correspond with the pulpit,
in a quartette, or at least in a paid organist, tenors
and sopranos. The pews must pay it all, and a
whole one needed by a journeyman mechanic for
himself and family will cost him as much yearly
rent as his house and garden before the war; unless he takes one below the respectable line, and
thereby shows every Sunday his lower social position.

But suppose, with his wife and three children,
he takes a fifty-dollar pew, that is, rents a second
house to worship in once a week, a still heavier tax
awaits him. Fashion, with all its quickly varying
and costly church styles, meets him on the threshold of the sacred and elegant building. This is the
last ounce that breaks or bends the back of his
ability. Fashion has got him fast now. By great
economy or additional industry he might stand a
fifty-dollar pew, and apparently rank with his better-
to-do neighbors. But he cannot bear this straining
burden of the pew and keep even with them with
the still heavier load of dress to equal their styles.
Here he must fall back into the rear. He and his
family must wear to church every Sunday, not the
" scarlet letter " of poverty, but an expressive badge
of their inferior position. We may blame him for
this sensibjlity, and call it pride, but not meanness.
It is a feeling that we cannot dissociate from

manliness, which no community can afford to contemn or ignore. Nor can we less admire and love our country because in no other one on the globe is this sensibility of working men so vivid and so easily touched. It is this sensitiveness, more than all other causes put together, that excludes so many thousands of that class from the churches in our large towns.

Thus we have the impressive fact before us, that here, even in our religious New England, there is no town of ten thousand inhabitants that has room in all its churches for over half its population. Still they are not filled by the other half. The supply follows the demand, but the demand for such a highly taxed luxury as religious worship in a costly and elegant church, is not forthcoming, nor is it expected when such churches are built.

Well, the workingman can, and does in thousands of cases, refuse to buy a pew or sit in a charity seat. He may, and often does, turn his back upon a fashionable church ; but he cannot turn his back upon a fashionable grave. There is no discharge for him from that condition. He must buy a family pew in the cemetery ; and when his soul is aflow on the flood-tide of its sorrow, the fashion of a modern funeral envelops it and him with its costly trappings and symbols of grief. His hands are hard with factory toil, but his heart is too soft to measure his means against that debt which others may think he owes to his dead. What if they should say that he thought of money at such an hour; that he kept back part of what was due to the worth and memory of his dead wife, son, or daughter! No; the sorrow of his broken spirit is a luxury which he must pay for, to those who witness it. He would not rent a fifty-dollar pew in the church, but he feels that he must now buy a fifty-dollar coffin for the dead mother of his children; then he must hire the regulation number of hacks for the real and professional mourners. The undertaker alone can tell him how many hacks should go to a fifty-dollar coffin. Then, although a cheap weed of grief will do for his own hat, he must put his daughters each in an entire mourning dress.

The funeral is over; he has complied in full with the unwritten rules of mourning which the city customs of religious sentiment prescribe. He goes back to his shop or factory and tries to work off the debt to the doctor and undertaker in the course of two years, besides supporting the residue of his family. But when he has paid the last dollar of the two bills, he has not done with the costly fashions of the grave. The memory of the dear one gone grows more and more tender in his heart, as he misses the light of that life in his own. And memory is a costly luxury which must be paid for, especially to the visitors to the cemetery, who never spoke to his wife while living, and have forgotten that she is dead. In a certain sense and

13

aspect, the modern cemetery is a more visible and permanent center of fashion than the church. The pews of the silent congregation cost more than its sittings. The social status of their holders is marked by more pronounced distinctions. The best pew in a fifty-thousand dollar church will not cost its richest worshiper more than one hundred dollars annual rent. He cannot make a great show of his wealth in his pew with any special upholstery, but he can do it in the cemetery to the full bent of his ambition. He erects a thousand or two thousand dollar monument over his family grave. He sets running a competitive race of social distinction among the grave-stones, high and low. Our journeyman mechanic feels that he must yield to the impulse. He has paid the doctor and undertaker, and now he must talk with the stone-cutter. He would stand well with public sentiment and custom. He would not be niggard towards a memory so dear to him. He agrees with the stone-cutter that a fifty-dollar monument is cheap enough for a fifty-dollar coffin and twelve hacks; so he orders one of that size and price for the grave of his wife.

Now, are not these things so? And is there no help for them? In every one of our cities and larger towns we see how the cost of Christian life and death, of the pew and the grave, is constantly increasing. Said a poor German mother to me, while dwelling upon the loveliness of a daughter she had buried: "We gave her a hundred and sixteen dollar funeral." Said a minister, with a salary of two thousand dollars : "If my wife should die in New York, and I should bury her in Greenwood cemetery with a funeral befitting my position, measured by public sentiment or custom, it would cripple me for life." Is it not time for thoughtful Christian men and women to come to the rescue of the Christian church and the Christian grave from the thraldom of fashions and customs that put such bars and burdens upon both.

SOME NEEDLESS ASPERITIES OF LIFE.

OMEBODY writing in an English magazine, has said, that the difference between a French and an English home, of the better class, lies mainly in the manner in which each seeks after its highest ideal excellence. In the French household, joy, gayety, mutual entertainment and the diversion of all, are the objects pursued. In the English, rest, leisure, the gratification of individual tastes, and the furtherance of individual aims, are regarded as chiefly important.

I have been thinking at what points the average American home touches either of these, and it seems to me not unfair to conclude that, commonly, neither rest nor joy set themselves before our families as desirable ends to be attained. Success in life, material prosperity, ambition in one or another form, allure us from our cradles onward. And our homes are merely convenient stopping places, to which we come jaded, from which we go refreshed, as, like campaigners in an enemy's country, we wage the incessant conflict against opposing circumstances. Happily we are gradually awakening to the fact that in too much labor there may be folly. And the new and generally diffused interest in household art is a good and favorable sign of the times. But the best of all household art is that which consists in making the household at ease, and pleased with itself and its members; and there are still chairs waiting at many hearths for the genial professors who shall teach its alphabet. A home, especially here, where everybody possesses the means of making his abode at least comfortable, and therefore attractive, should be more than a mere inn for the feeding of hungry guests, or a lodging-house, where they may find beds when they are weary.

That it is sometimes no more than this, is abundantly proved by observation. We see brothers and sisters, and sons and daughters, who are in haste to find any shelter, rather than that of the parental roof. We know that people often yawn by their own firesides, while they are quite brilliant abroad.

We reluctantly admit that sparkle, flavor and charm, the zest of life, is not invariably found, even in homes which are hallowed in the morning and at night by the breath of sincere devotion. We cannot fail to see, that life may be honest, honorable, useful and charitable, and withal, intensely disagreeable; so that, till relieved from its needless asperities, its cup at the lips shall be bitter, and its memories in the heart be like bells out of tune.

Foremost, among the deplorable distresses which

disturb domestic peace, is the vice of fault-finding.
It matters very little who the inveterate fault-finder
is.   If it be a parent, it is rather worse than if it
be one of the children, for parents are always entitled to respect, and nobody can satisfactorily resent
their unjust criticisms.   Perhaps the transgressors
are almost unaware of the extent of their sin, for
the bad habit of scolding began long ago, and
being tolerated, has become unconscious.   Men
and women may scold, and scowl, and sneer, and
yet believe themselves patterns of amiability.
There are tables at which the sauce to every dish is
the same.   The fish is watery, the potatoes are
soggy, the meats are over or underdone, the gravies
are burned, and the pastry is heavy.   Nothing is
right.   At such feasts the saying of grace is a manifest irony.

It may not be a fault-finder, but only a melancholy and moody young lady or gentleman, whose
views of the world are all colored by dyspepsia, or
hypochondria, who manages to make home gloomy
and wretched.   Companionship with one who is
morbid or cynical, as with one who is often perverse and quarrelsome, occasions a friction which is
very wearing.   In the home afflicted by the presence of any of these unfortunates, the days never
glide by.   They bump along, with a succession of
jolts, like springless carts over a corduroy road.
No wonder people lie down tired at night, to waken
hopeless in the morning, with so much to tax
patience and Christian resignation.

A frequent and needless asperity is found in the
lack of that sturdy independence, which accepts
the situation, and adjusts arrangements to it with
dignity. You cannot afford to dwell in a certain
street, nor to maintain a certain style, and of this
you feel assured. Your income, provided your
expenses could be reduced, would amply suffice for
comfort, while, as it is, the prophet's simile fits
your case precisely, for the bed is too short, and the
coverlets are too narrow. It is humiliating to pride
to make changes which will tell friends and neighbors that one has been unfortunate, or injudicious;
and so you go on, burdened with care, worried by
demands which you cannot meet, and which
increase in proportion to your inability. Now,
there is neither sense nor wisdom in carrying loads
which diminish strength, and add nothing to
growth in grace. All reasonable persons must be
convinced, on reflection, that life is too brief to
be wasted in the struggles to keep up a vain show.
What have we to do with self-imposed vexations?
Is not the life more than meat? Shall it not possess some freedom, some margin, some elasticity?
We desire breathing-spaces, mountain-tops, room
for friends, and room for our own souls, and we
cannot have them, if the demon of debt be forever
dogging our steps.

Another source of unprofitable sorrow arises
from fancied slights and neglects, and from small
misunderstandings. Too much importance ought

never to be attached to these. We should not be too sensitive for comfort. We should not too tenaciously watch over our personal dignity. The trivial things which destroy our composure, and invade our peace, are pitiful. An acquaintance is preoccupied, and passes us with a hurried recognition on the street; another fails to return our call, or seems to prefer the society of some one else to ours, and we are harrowed and hurt. Jealousy is the discontent of outraged love, not only, it is the hateful child of envy and covetousness. It is not too mean to be displayed by a petted animal, or by an aggravated baby. Ignorant women nourish it in the breasts of little ones under their care, not dreaming of the harm they are doing. Through the years of a human life, there can be no passion so allied to the serpent-brood of evil, as this half-insane trait of jealousy.

So often must we sit beneath the shadow, so often shed the tears of bereavement and regret, and so often toil upward bearing the cross, that we should court no useless rigors. Let us always welcome the sunshine. Let us be receptive to all that is gracious and winning. Let us be happy ourselves and make others so. It is the brave heart which is the cheery one. Suffering, for suffering's sake only, is not meritorious. To shiver in a dungeon, when there is a south wind blowing, and flowers are abloom in the spring warmth, is to behave like an idiot, and not like a saint. Count

that day **lost,** in which you have not **made** a child
gladder, nor **given a** delight **to your beloved, nor**
blessed the mourner **by your gentleness.** There
must be offenses, but **the** Saviour's **words stand:**
" Woe unto him **by whom the offense cometh!** "

TOIL AND REST.

WHEN sets the weary sun,
And the long day is done,
And starry orbs their solemn vigils keep;
When bent with toil and care,
We breathe our evening prayer,
God gently giveth His beloved sleep.

.   .   .   .

And when life's day shall close
In death's last deep repose,
When the dark shadows o'er the eyelids creep;
Let us not be afraid,
At this thick gathering shade,
For so God giveth His beloved sleep.

To die? it is to rise
To fairer, brighter skies,
Where death no more shall his dread harvests reap;
To soar on angel wings,
Where life immortal springs,
For so He giveth His beloved sleep.

JOSEPH HERON'S RESOLUTION.

———

"Tell us something that really happened." — *Boys and Girls.*

"And so I will." — *Mary Morrison.*

JOSEPH Heron lived in Reedsville. He was a plain, freckled-faced boy, rather small of his age, and with an unfortunate habit of stammering. He was a quiet, bashful boy, but faithful to his widowed mother, and industrious in his school. There was one trial Joseph had, which to him was the greatest; this was school declamation.

He had never forgotten how the boys laughed that afternoon when he "spoke Casabianca."

"The b–boy st–st–ood on the b–b–burning d–deck,
Whence all b–b–ut him had f-f-f—"

"I think they must have had hard work f-f-lee-ing," whispered Bob Jones, so loud that Joseph could but hear, and the blood rushed to his face.

Then Hal Perkins, to whom the remark was made, laughed aloud, and poor Joe stopped discour-aged and went to his seat. Since this first time,

his teacher had given him private lessons, and he
had tried to improve; he had just begun to do
better, still nothing seemed so difficult to him as to
declaim.

The past winter there had been much religious
interest in the church which Joseph and his mother
attended, and many of Joe's friends had made a
firm resolve to serve the Lord.

One night Joe went home from prayer-meeting
and found his mother sewing, as usual, by the little
kerosene lamp in the kitchen. He went in, and,
drawing a low seat up by her, said:

"Mother, dear, Mr. Jameson told us to—n—night
the—the story of Joshua's resolution. 'As for me
and my house, we will serve the Lord,' and he
t—told us we m—might any of us then and there
m—make the same resolution for ourselves. And
then he s—said to us, 'Choose ye th—this day whom
ye will serve.' It seemed t—to me as if the Lord
was s—speaking right to m—me, and I thought the
people must hear m—my heart beat; b—but it was
only a f—few m—minutes; mother, I made up my
mind. I chose!"

"Is it possible, my dear boy," said the widow, as
the tears fell fast on the unfinished garment in her
lap; "have *you* chosen to serve the Lord?"

"Yes, mother; 'as for m—me, I will,' God helping m—me; and what is m—more, to-morrow n—night
when the minister calls on th—those who have
resolved, to t—t—testify of their hopes, I m—mean
to tell of mine."

" You are not afraid of stammering, Joe ? "

" No, m—mother ; I feel sure th—the Lord will help m—me."

" But, my love, think how hard it is for you to declaim at school ; and think how much harder it will be to speak there."

" I'm n—not afraid, mother."

Truly, thought Mrs. Heron, this is the grace of God.

The next evening, at the prayer-meeting, little, pale Mrs. Heron, on the women's side, listened tremblingly for a weak, stammering voice, but the one she loved above all others on earth.

Mr. Jameson said, when the meeting was half over : " I repeat the request I made at the beginning, that those who have lately chosen to serve the Lord, testify."

Joseph Heron rose. Poor Mrs. Heron's heart was in her mouth, and she had hidden her face in her handkerchief. Joseph, pale, resolute, looked about on the assembly an instant ; there were the boys who laughed at Casabianca ; there was the great preacher, at least he seemed a " son of thunder " to poor Joe, and then the people were all so still, nothing but the ticking of the clock to be heard, all waiting to hear *him.* Just then he caught sight of his mother, in deep black, bent over, her face in her hands. He took courage.

" My friends," he said in a full, clear voice, " I have made up my mind that as for me I will serve the Lord. It was only last night that I made this resolution, but the day past has been the happiest of my life." Here, poor little Mrs. Heron's handkerchief fell from her eyes. Could this be her Joe! He did not stammer; she even took courage to look.

Joe went on : " I want to ask all my young friends to serve the Lord too. It is a glorious service, and the wages are everlasting life."

Joseph sat down, and others followed; but no one attracted so much interest as he. It seemed as if then and there the Lord had wrought a miracle. Every word had been full, clear, and distinct, uttered without hesitation. Even Joe himself was as surprised as any of them. But after service, as Joe walked home with his mother, his stammering had returned. But when he knelt to pray with her, after reading the Bible, lo, the clear, unhesitating voice came back.

" It is the gift of the Lord, mother," said Joe. " I thought it would be s—so hard to speak or p—pray in meeting, and I prayed to Him to give me strength ; and this is th—the way He will do it. I shall n—never be afraid now to witness for Him in the m—meeting. He has n—not given m—me the power in every th—thing, but just f—for Him. It is wrong, I suppose, mother ; but I am troubled about tomorrow. I am afraid all the boys will l—laugh at me and sneer, and ask me if I've t—taken to e—exhorting."

"Yes, Joseph," said his mother; "you are wrong in being afraid. Ask God to help you, and He will; but even if you are 'reproached for His name,' the Bible says, 'happy are ye.'"

So Joseph went to school the next day, braced up for an attack, but ready for conflict; ready, in other words, to take patiently any unkind or cruel things that might be said. His mother watched for him rather anxiously at noon. The pine table was covered with a coarse brown linen cloth, the Indian mush was smoking in the dish, and Mrs. Heron was taking a few stitches in her work, as she sat waiting for her son.

The door was suddenly thrown open, and Joe's face, wreathed in smiles, appeared.

"Well, my boy, come, sit down, dinner is smoking hot. You have not had a *very* hard time to-day, have you?"

"I–I–I don't know wh–what possessed the b–boys, mother. They were n–never so kind in th–their lives; and wh–what do you th–think? Hal Perkins came to m–me, and a–asked my p–pardon for a–all his u–ugliness, a–and h–he says he is g–going to try and be a Christian, too, and w–wants me to help him."

"And it came to pass," said Mrs. Heron, "'when Christian came near where the lions were, behold they were chained!'"

" I HAVE CALLED YOU FRIENDS."

FROM the fine fret of little care,
  That gnaweth bitterly
Upon the soul grown sore to it,
  I turn, O Christ! to Thee.
O Thou, the Careworn! can'st Thou turn
  As longingly to me?

Worn with the deeper wear of sin
  Graven on the soul of me;
In such a marred and shattered thing,
  O perfect Heart! can'st see
A nature fit by any cost
  To be a *friend* to Thee?

Is that the meaning of the Word
  Which says Thou *lovest* me?
By the deep stirring of my heart
  In yearning after Thee,
By all the longing of the life
  That leaneth unto Thee,

As human friend with human friend,
  Can I so think of Thee?
Like human love with human love
  Will heavenly rapture be?
Such more than human blessedness
  Be meant in truth for me!

HOW THE QUESTION WAS ANSWERED.

THIS sketch, which aims to recall a simple tale of actual experience, begins at a time when the writer was the pastor of a church in a Western city. In a certain circle of our young men, Egbert L—— was the acknowledged head and leader. He was a person of active mind and agreeable manners. He was a ready and versatile talker. Considerable reading of both orthodox and skeptical writers had made him rather apt in religious discussion, of which he was fond. His seemingly careful and candid way of looking into the great questions of the human soul, gave all the greater plausibility to his opinions in the eyes of his young friends and admirers. Though he invariably took the side of unbelief, he knew how to keep his temper in debate, and to treat even the most indignant opponent with courtesy. I had heard of him as a person of decided mental resource, who was exerting a dangerous influence over some young men of my own congregation. Yet I never sought him out. What to do in such a case has taxed the best wisdom of many an anxious pastor. Pride of opinion is so often the principal stock in trade of an embryo infidel, that it becomes a serious question whether direct personal effort will really explode the bubble, or only still further distend it. At all events, whether wisely or unwisely, I did not interfere.

When at length I was called to unite Mr. L—— in marriage with a young lady of my flock, it did not occur to me even then that any future interest would hinge on so ordinary a circumstance. There was indeed a tinge of sadness in the thought that the union which I was thus called to solemnize had not in it that which ought always to sweeten so dear a bond, namely, the supreme joy of an infinite prospect. But business would soon lead him to make his home in another State; and so, when I joined their hands in one, and with words of blessing dismissed them for the wedding journey, it was with the thought that that brief hour of the nuptial scene was probably the ending, as it had been the beginning, of my acquaintance with Mr. L——.

It was a surprise, therefore, when a few months later, a long letter came with his name appended. The contents of the letter were even more surprising. That letter lies before me now as I write these lines. It informed me that he had been overtaken by a strange event. A change had occurred in his feelings such as he had never supposed could possibly happen, at least to him. And that change had come about in a manner so remarkable that he

14

could not account for it otherwise than by suppos‧
ing it to be the work of a supernatural power.

Business, he says, had called him to the wilds of
northern Minnesota. Walking alone one day
through the deep woods for the purpose of viewing
some timber which he had purchased, he fell into
what was to him an unwonted path of meditation.
Under those tall and solemn pines his past life ‑
began to march in review before the eye of his
memory. Scenes and events came back with all
the freshness of yesterday. His brain seemed pre-
ternaturally quickened. The *impression* of all that
passed in his mind was of a kind that no mental
retrospect had ever produced on him before.
Briefly stated, the substance of his thoughts
seemed to have been, that during the years of his
life he had received many good things, for all of
which he had never yet expressed any gratitude to
the Infinite Giver.

Such a reflection might seem ordinary enough,
indeed; but at this time it somehow acquired
a strange power. It pierced his very soul like
the thrust of a javelin. It literally felled him
to the ground. How it was he hardly knew, but
he found himself on his knees at the foot of a tree,
uttering loud cries and broken prayers to God for
mercy and forgiveness.

In the letter before me L—— does not say that
he was distinctly conscious of becoming a changed
man while thus prostrate in that solemn sanctuary

of nature, or what precise meaning he connected with the feelings which had so suddenly overpowered him.   But he *did* remember in that very hour of spiritual tumult, that he had often boasted that such a thing could never come to *him!*   Unquestionably, therefore, it had the effect to chasten his conceit, and to open his mind to a wholly new set of opinions.   He had become willing all at once to look at some things as he never had done before.

It was considerably past nightfall when L—— returned to the camp which he had left when he went out to count the " stumpage " which he had purchased.   But among the rough lumbermen who had come in from the day's chopping he saw no one to whom he felt inclined to tell the strange experience which had marked the day as the most memorable of his life.   A few days later he had occasion to visit the nearest city on the river below.   On reaching the bustling town, something prompted him to inquire for the reading-room of the Young Men's Christian Association.   Perhaps it was a vague hope of meeting there some one to whom he might venture to mention his new feelings.   Instead, however, of the coveted opportunity, he found what was still better.

On entering the reading-room, his eye rested first on the Bible that lay on the table amidst reviews, newspapers, and magazines.   That he should not deem it necessary to glance just at the morning paper, struck him as another strange thing added to the many that were being clustered together in his new experience. But so it was, somehow, and the wealth of periodicals about him had no attraction for him that morning; but a singular impulse led him straight to that Bible — a volume whose leaves he had turned before, indeed, but he could hardly remember when. At the page where he first opened, he began to read. What now ? What electric spell had taken possession of those familiar types? What hidden talisman in those pages is it, whose mighty finger have laid hold of his very heartstrings ? When before did he ever find himself held to that Book as by the glittering eye of a charmer ? With strange eagerness he keeps on reading. Hours pass, and still he reads. When at length he returns to the consciousness of his mundane relations, and a quick glance at his watch reminds him of a business engagement, his first thought is that this new experience with the Bible is hardly less wonderful to him than that other wonderful experience that had come to him in the deep solitude of the pine forest only a few days before.

Every day, he writes me, he visited that reading-room, so long as his business detained him in the city. And each day his whole leisure time was occupied, not with the files of papers, but in pondering those precious sentences of eternal wisdom. And every day, he adds, it was to him a theme of increasing amazement that his mind could ever have been dull to a volume of such unfathomable interest and wealth.

At length, one day, as he sits reading in his accustomed place, he observes that the room is being taken possession of by an audience of men. It is the business men's weekly prayer-meeting. He closes his book and listens. He had heard prayers and hymns before, but never with such sensations as now. To-day, as these songs arise, and as those petitions go forth with thrilling fervor from the hearts of those earnest men, it is to our Egbert the unveiling of a new world. Tears pour down his cheeks like rain. He sees now for himself that the armor of his old-time obstinacy on religious subjects is pierced, broken, and shattered. Even *he* is melted by a prayer-meeting — even he, the proud Egbert L——, who had often ranked such an assembly in the same catalogue with the incantations of a Hottentot! That prayer-meeting was to him a place of discovery. In the light of that hour it was that he opened his eyes at last to the tokens of a change in himself.

Before the meeting is ended, it is impressed on him that he ought to tell these good men what has lately happened to him. With such self-mastery as he can command, he rises and begins. He has hardly finished before he is greeted with a tumult of sympathy. There is no chance for benediction or any formal closing of the meeting, so many of the men have left their seats to gather about him

with handshakings and words of Christian recognition. This letter assures me that never till that
moment did he know what a sweet thing was meant
by that New Testament word, " fellowship."

It was shortly after this prayer-meeting scene
that this letter was written, in which L——
describes to me the wondrous way in which the
Lord had led him. It was on Wednesday that
the letter reached me. Of course I accepted it as
a special message for my own prayer-meeting of
that evening. And indeed it proved so. It fell on
our evening gathering like a thunder-clap from a
clear sky. Could it be possible ? Egbert L——
actually converted, and in such a wonderful way!
The Spirit's presence was already being felt among
my people, and this news only deepened the impression. A few of the young men, however, who had
been intimate companions of Egbert, could hardly
credit the tidings. They would not believe till
they saw and heard from his own lips. They were
not long denied the opportunity. Very unexpect-
edly word came that L—— would be with us for
only a brief stop on a certain day. A meeting was
quickly arranged at the house of one of his old
friends. He was there at the time appointed. It
was an hour and a scene which I shall never forget.
In the presence of a crowded room full of sobbing
listeners, I saw him stand up and tell in his own
direct and simple and manly way, how God had
brought him out of great darkness into marvelous

light. Among the points in his remarks which I distinctly recall, he said in substance this : " My friends, some of you will remember that I used to say that conversion was only a physical excitement; that it was the product of a crowded room, of hot air, and the magnetic contact of mind with mind; that the Lord had nothing to do with it; that it was easy enough for men to convert each other at any time, if they only knew enough to supply the proper mental and mechanical conditions. I am not sure but I honestly thought so. But I thank God for showing me my mistake; and I thank Him with all my heart for doing it just as He did — taking me out into those woods, away off up there at the head-waters of the Mississippi, a hundred miles beyond the homes of civilized men, leading me out alone into His own solemn temple of nature, where there was no eye but God's to see me, no voice but God's to speak to me — I praise Him that there in that solitary stillness He laid His hand upon me and pressed me to the earth under a sense of the sins and ingratitude of my life; and that there He showed me at last that, not simply the work of man, but the power of the Highest, has something to do in this matter of religion. I am convinced, my friends; I am convinced."

These words were uttered with an intensity of feeling that lifted the speaker almost to a pitch of eloquence. They carried conviction to others also, even the most skeptical. Yes, it was impossible to doubt longer. The great change had really come to Egbert L——, and for him too had been answered the most momentous question of the human soul.

LOVE'S ESTIMATE.

SMOOTH shells and rounded pebbles from the beach,
   With coral sprays from sunny isles afar,
Lie on the mantel out of baby's reach.
   She, thinking these my choicest treasures are,
Digs diligently with her dimpled hands
For rough rock fragments in the common sands,
   And ranges them upon a lower shelf.
   "Pitties for mamma.   Finded 'em myself!"
I kiss the lifted forehead, and I make
Treasures of worthless things for baby's sake.

So God loves us.   From ranks of Seraphim
He stoops to take the gifts we offer Him.
He knows our weakness, ignorance and sin,
He views our offerings as they should have been.

THE SALEM SUFFERER.

T is wonderful how little outward circumstances have to do with one's happiness! "A good man shall be satisfied from himself," so it was said some three thousand years ago; and three thousand years have continually illustrated its truth. The only satisfying spring is inside.

When I was a child, my father used to take me with him in his pious calls on a poor, bedridden young woman in my native city. While still on the pavement below, I would hear sounds that made me shudder; and I shuddered the more as I saw her, in the partially darkened room, start up suddenly into a sitting posture, beat her right hand violently against her face, and fling herself back against a rubber sheet stretched near the wall at her head.

These spasms occurred every few minutes, day and night, so that there was no possibility of proper sleep; nor was there any, except that toward morning a slight feeling of stupor would come over her, not, however, locking up a single sense.

Nor was this all. The violence of her blows had

wholly destroyed the sight of one eye. Painful
ulcers found vent at her ears. Bloody matter was
expectorated from her lungs. Worse than all, her
throat was in such a condition that *she could eat
absolutely nothing.* And the little nourishment she
took in a liquid form seemed even about to strangle
her to death!

Can one think of more downright misery — the
sources of happiness more completely cut off?
Literally unable to eat or sleep! and strangulation
instead of the pleasure of appetite at every mouth-
ful swallowed.

But I, who saw her thus when a boy, saw her the
same, and very many times too, when a man. I
went through a long preparation for college ; pursued a college course ; spent two years in teaching,
and then three at the theological seminary ; again
taught two years ; next served three years as a
pastor ; and then entered on a long professorship,
sometime during which the sufferer entered on the
rest of heaven.

Through all these years of growth and change
and work — that seemed an age — as I thought of
her, every day and every night was like every other,
save that the dreadful monotony tended to worse
and worse, with paroxysms far more powerful,
which either for months doubled her up like a half-
closed knife, or threw her suddenly far out upon
the floor. Indeed, release came from a deadly blow
inflicted in one of these latter spasms.

During that score of years — will my readers believe me? — if one had asked me to lead him to the happiest heart I knew in the city of Salem, Mass., I should have taken him to that dear sufferer, always, when not in a spasm, sunny, always trustful, always loving,. always grateful, always thoughtful of others, always ready with a sweet word for her Saviour! To other sick chambers I have gone to carry spiritual consolation, but to hers never. In her was the "well of water springing up into everlasting life," refreshing her own soul and perpetually overflowing in abundant streams to others.

Said one of her physicians to me — physicians visited her from all parts of the world — "Sarah Purbeck is the most wonderful illustration of the power of religion to sustain, I have ever known or read of."

How does such a case prove the possibility of a soul-life wholly independent of the life of the body ; and that Jesus Christ is the true life of the soul.

SOCIALISM IN GERMANY.

THERE is no distinct point nor act to mark the rise of Socialism in Germany as a practical question of government and society. Here and there a speculative professor or a dreamy philosopher had put forth a Socialistic scheme of society as a fantasy of his own brain, with hardly a thought of its ever being reduced to experiment in practical life. But such fantasies, when seized upon by the common mind, have been dangerous incentives to social revolution ; and the more dangerous in the degree that they were chimerical. When philosophers go mad, what follies may not be expected from the people ? But though philosophers had tinged the common mind with the illusion of a Socialistic paradise, hunger first roused the people to a war upon society in behalf of labor. The introduction of machinery into Germany caused, in certain departments of labor, a revolution so sudden and complete that masses of workmen were thrown out of employment. These began to assail capital as their enemy, and to call upon government for relief. This was especially the case with the hand-weavers of Silesia,

nearly forty years ago, whose riotous outbreaks
against factories required to be put down by military force. Some writers date the Socialistic movement from that event.

But that was really a wild uprising of men
threatened with famine, and not the attempt to
realize any political or Socialistic scheme of reform.
Socialism was a malaria which slowly infected the
body politic, but did not manifest itself by outward
symptoms until a feverish condition of the atmosphere brought it out with sudden and alarming
virulence ; and this was only within the last twenty
years. This social disease originated in France,
and passed into Germany, at first through the
medium of political revolution, which originated in
quite other grounds. The revolutionary spirit,
which in 1848 spread from France to Europe, gave
a new impulse to the hopes of the Liberals in Germany, but had little to do with the emancipation of
labor through a social democracy. In Germany the
common people, for ages accustomed to subjection,
had hardly come to the consciousness of political
life, and the dream of democracy was scattered by
the reaction which followed the frenzy of '48.

But though the agitation was suppressed, at least
in its open and violent forms, it had stirred the
masses of society with new hopes for their future.
In place of dreamy philosophers, practical leaders
arose, with a faculty for organization and powers of
popular appeal. Chief among these were Karl

Marx, who, after the suppression of revolution in 1849, went over to the extremest doctrines of French Socialism; and Ferdinand Lassalle, who, when things were quieted down in Prussia, conceived the project of drilling workmen into a political party aiming at the overthrow of capital, through workingmen's associations, and the reconstruction of society through the polls. Marx reduced Socialism to a philosophical system; Lassalle endowed it with the gift of organization, and thus inspired it with the consciousness of power in asserting its own demands. Both these leaders commanded attention by their rare intellectual ability. Lassalle especially was heard and read with respect even by the upper-classes, and his earlier schemes for the relief of workmen, being regarded as more philanthropic than political, were at first aided by the Prussian government. Bismarck at one time coquetted with Lassalle as a possible ally in his own political and social schemes. Through these writers and their colleagues the most advanced doctrines of French Socialists were made familiar to the common people of Germany.

With the growth of manufactures came a large increase of the artisan class in Germany, in contrast to the agricultural, which had hitherto formed the bulk of the laboring population. As a rule in all countries, Socialism gathers its adherents not from the men who till the soil, but from artisans in cities, towns and manufacturing villages. These have interests in common, and have facilities for intercourse and organization which lay them open to the influence of demagogues and to the propagation of novel ideas. Events in Germany, and especially in Prussia, from 1860 to 1871, favored the growth of political power among workmen. Under the constitution of Prussia, there was already an extended popular suffrage, and when the struggle for supremacy arose between the government and the Parliament, the workmen's vote, which went almost as a unit, was courted both by Liberals and by Conservatives as a balance of power. But the constitution of the North German Confederation, and afterwards that of the German Empire, made suffrage absolutely universal — every German twenty-five years of age, and neither a pauper nor a criminal, being entitled to vote by ballot and without challenge for members of Parliament. Of course, workmen were now a power in politics in the exact proportion of their numbers, and by giving their united strength to a single purpose, could make that power felt. The Socialist leaders were prompt to avail themselves of this immense facility, by a thorough organization and an active drill of the social democracy.

In 1871, the German army returned victorious from France, bringing with it the unity which Republicans and Revolutionists had struggled for in vain, and also an enormous sum of money, with which to set up the new Empire. Everybody went wild. Henceforth Germany was the head of Europe, not only in power but in plenty and prosperity. Workmen in the country, and in the mines, left their drudgery and hurried to the cities to pick up gold in the streets. Buildings went up by magic, new banks were formed, railways projected, factories started, towns laid out; in a word, society was turned upside down to prepare for the millennium of labor. In Berlin I then saw the workman at his four and five dollars a day, instead of riding as formerly, by omnibus or tramway, or trudging along with his tools, driving to and from his work in a first-class hack, with his jolly comrades, singing and shouting. Having been taught that all which society is, and has, is " the creation of labor," and having now money and votes, why should not workmen reconstruct the world to suit themselves?

That was the heyday of Socialistic theories, and the leaders now aimed at Parliament as the theater for acting out their views. But the crash of 1873, and the prolonged state of business depression not yet relieved, brought down the workman from these high places to struggle again with those forces of nature and society which he can neither resist nor understand. For a time he attempted to resist by strikes; but being compelled to succumb to the inevitable, he began to talk of revolution, and, as before, to look upon society as his enemy. There were occasional outbreaks, but in face of a huge standing army it was idle to think of a revolution by force. The workman, however, had tasted of luxury, and had learned his political power, and, by appealing to his passions and his ambition, the Socialistic leaders now labored the more earnestly to increase the party, which should overturn society through the force of a majority.

Such, in brief, has been the course of the Socialistic movement in Germany — wild theories of political economy taken up by the masses as their gospel; able and eloquent demagogues accepted by the masses as their oracles; financial inflation giving them a taste of luxury, and political suffrage a dream of power; then the sudden sharp reverse of fortune, hard times, low wages and want and misery consequent upon their own extravagance. Add to these the doctrine in which Germans have always been trained, that the State makes and unmakes society at will, and nothing could be more natural than the notion of ignorant and inexperienced men, that if they could set aside the State, or control it, they could satisfy all their desires. The pressure of taxes and of a vast military and civil organization above them lends a touch of pity to the very madness of their dream.

15

MR. THOMPSON'S SIN.

LAM Thompson was a farmer. His residence was in the outskirts of a town among the hills of New England. In one corner of the town was a railroad station on one of the leading lines of the State. The corporation offered a fair price for wood, and many of the farmers of the town furnished large quantities. In fact, some of them made it their principal business to cut and, draw wood. Of this class was Mr. Thompson, who hired Canadians to chop the wood, while he drew it from the farm to the station.

Mr. Ensign had the care of the railroad station. To him the treasurer of the company remitted funds, and commissioned him not only to measure the wood, but to pay for the same. It happened that on one occasion a large amount of money was due to individuals who had been drawing wood. On a pleasant day in March, Mr. Thompson came to the station for his pay for several hundred cords of wood. He was invited into the office to receive his money. While engaged in computing the amount due him, a train arrived, and the station agent stepped upon the platform for a few moments, leaving **Mr. Thompson** standing by the desk, where bills **were lying in packages** of one **hundred and two hundred dollars. After finding the amount due to Mr. Thompson, the agent paid him, and he took** his **leave. After his departure Mr. Ensign counted his money, and found the amount two hundred dollars short. Several persons had** been settled **with that day. He** referred **to his** memorandum-book, and carefully examined the amount each had been paid, and then over **and** over again he counted the packages of money. **He was** satisfied that **no** mistake had been made in his computation, **and that he had unwittingly paid some person two** hundred **dollars too much, or that some one had** taken **that amount of money. He was quite confident that when Mr. Thompson came for his pay the cash was all right.**

The station master settled with the corporation, and made up the deficit **from his own pocket. It was perfectly** natural **that Mr.** Ensign **should** suppose that **Mr.** Thompson **took that money;** but he was **a prudent man, and** because **he** could not *prove* **the theft, he concluded** that the wiser course was **to keep** silence, and **leave** it to the future **to make the matter** plain. **He could not very easily make up his mind that Mr. Thompson would do** . **such an act. He was a member of the church, ánd was considered very respectable. He had never been** charged with **any such offense, and for this reason it** was **difficult for Mr.** Ensign to believe **that he would commit such a crime.**

It should have been stated at the outset that when Mr. Thompson purchased his land he could not pay the full amount. His "wood money," so-called, by special agreement, was to go towards paying for his farm. Had Mr. Ensign discovered that he had paid more than usual on the mortgage, he would have been more fully satisfied that he had taken the money. He made inquiry, and found that he had paid only the same amount as usual. Thus while his suspicions were strong, there seemed to be no *positive* proof that they were well grounded; and yet Mr. Ensign had not a doubt that Mr. Thompson took the money.

One year passed after another. Mr. Thompson drew wood to the station, and received his pay for it, and at length became free from debt. During all this time there was no allusion made to the two hundred dollars that had been missed. Mr. Ensign began to call in question the truthfulness of his own suspicions, and to think that, perhaps, he had judged uncharitably. He had, however, done what very few men would have done in his circumstances. He had never told any person — even his wife — that he suspected Mr. Thompson of theft.

Meanwhile, how was it with Mr. Thompson? He knew that Mr. Ensign regarded him with suspicion. Still he never alluded to the matter in any of their dealings. He allowed himself to go along, maintaining outwardly his profession of religion, but destitute, in large measure, of enjoyment. His sin was ever before him. He felt that he could not bear to have the finger of scorn pointed at him. He concealed his guilt. He did not dare tell his wife. He treasured up in his own soul the terrible secret. It gnawed there like the worm. It burned there like the fire. He never had a happy day after he put that two hundred dollars in his pocket. Sometimes he was determined to take it and send it back without communicating from whom it came. Why did he not? Alas, he loved money, and he could not bear to part with it.

The time came at length when God revealed his sin. He was taken sick. Now his conscience was aroused in an unwonted manner. To him it seemed that on the ceiling, and on the side walls of his bedroom, was inscribed in glowing letters, *two hundred dollars.* " Alas," said he, " alas, that I should have sold my soul for the paltry sum of two hundred dollars."

He called his hired man to his bedside and said : " Go for the doctor, and ask him to come at once. When he has been seen, go to Mr. Ensign, and tell him I would like to have him come up here. I want to see him on some important business."

The physician came and examined his patient, and could not make out that he was afflicted with any serious sickness, only that he was very nervous. He prescribed an anodyne and left. Soon Mr. Ensign reached the house. Mr. Thompson requested all to leave the room except his visitor.

He invited him to sit close by his bed. He then
reached out his hand and said: "Can you take
hold of a hand that has done you such wrong?
I stole two hundred dollars from you, and I have
sent for you that I may confess it and make reparation."

Mr. Ensign took his hand and said: "Mr.
Thompson, how could you do that act, and sin
against God?"

"Well, sir, it was because the devil tempted me.
I was in debt. I wanted money to pay for my
place. I felt that the corporation had not done the
fair thing in docking off fifty cents a cord on some
of my wood. I knew the corporation was rich, and
would never miss the money. I took it; but I did
not dare to pay it in toward my farm. I did not
dare tell my wife that I had taken it. I carried it
to —— and deposited it in the savings bank. It is
there now. I have never drawn a cent of it out.
Principal and interest are all there. It belongs to
you. You have never charged me with the theft
as I have ever heard, and for that reason no one
but God and you and I know of the sin. And
now can you forgive me? If the money in the
bank is not sufficient pecuniary reparation, I will
make it more."

"I could not at first believe," said Mr. Ensign,
"you would do such an act; but I could not
account for the two hundred dollars without sus-
pecting you. Inasmuch, however, as you express

penitence, I will forgive you. I must say one thing, and that is that the firm persuasion I have had that you took that money has led me to doubt whether there was any reality in religion. Now that you have confessed and proffered ample reparation for your sin, I feel differently. If you had died and made no sign, I should probably have gone to my grave with the feeling that all religion, so-called, was a sham."

"My dear sir, don't charge my crime to religion. It was committed by me when Satan tempted me. God give you and me grace to break away from his devices, and walk in the fear of God. I have made my will, and have devised to you all moneys standing to my credit in the savings bank in ——. My executors will see that you are paid."

Mr. Ensign said : "Your executors will not carry out your good intentions for years to come. You will be on your feet again in a few days. I met the doctor and asked him what ailed you, and he said it was more trouble of mind than anything else ; and now that this has been removed by your own act, you will soon be able to go to —— and do this business yourself. If you wish, all that has passed between us now shall remain a secret. I trust we shall learn by this terrible fall, and the pain it has occasioned, to pray ' Lead us not into temptation.' Good-day, Mr. Thompson."

It was as the doctor had said, and as Mr. Ensign had predicted ; Mr. Thompson was soon able to be about. He got his money from the bank and paid Mr. Ensign, so that he was satisfied. He never told his wife how he had well-nigh gone down to perdition.

AMBITION.

THE wise have ever held ambition's gains
  As worse than worthless, since these fail to give
  The meed whereby the dying hopes to live.
Alas! such gathers for his life-long pains
But a poor, mortal benefit, that wanes
  Before the years, as sands drop through a sieve,
  While angels looking on must surely grieve
Over a soul that nothing more attains:
Over a soul that, with an equal leaven
  Of high endeavor set to holier theme
Than this, to which its restlessness was given —
  Just to the following of love's peaceful stream —
Might now be conscious of a present heaven,
  And reap immortal life beyond its dream!

A CHAPTER OF ACCIDENTS.

HAVE found out that a man may be actuated by excellent motives, and be perfectly sincere in his belief, and calculate to do about as well as he can, and be in many respects painstaking and prudent in pursuing his course, and at the same time he may be greatly mistaken, and may involve himself in serious difficulties.

I went to the Northern depot in Lowell on a Saturday night, with what I thought a good motive, to preach in Ashland next day. Feeling a little inclined to put blame on somebody, after the manner of those who accuse an unknown origin of evil, or Adam, I really suppose that the general manager of the Boston, Lowell and Nashua Railroad, and all the people of Lowell, are at the bottom of my mishaps; for everybody knows that there ought to be a new depot, and that there would have been, if it had not been sagaciously promised to build one whenever the citizens should agree where to put it. If they had agreed, or he had built it on his own judgment, you would have been spared this article. The uninviting accommodations led me to take refuge in an arm-chair in the express office, rather than occupy one of the regular rooms, or pace up and down the platform waiting for the train.

Again, my sincerity and intention to do about right stood in my way. I was sincere in the belief that the Framingham cars would back down ten or fifteen feet further than they did, because they had usually done it; and if that had been done you would have escaped this infliction of my accidents. And I thought I did about right in looking sharply down the track two minutes before the train ought to start, and then, not seeing it, to sit down in said arm-chair to wait patiently. And, with prudence, I took my seat near an open window about opposite where the train usually starts. But I was very much intent on writing a few sentences in my note-book; so that, in fault of the usual movements of the train, and the usual outcries which I did not hear, I was left. My main business, however, in being at that station was to get that train; and I had no right to get absorbed in finishing my sermon, or to trust to the railroad routine; and if I had carried my eyes and ears about instead of seating them, you would not have heard from me. I was like a man so engrossed in the cares or pleasures of this life as to be unheeding of the alarms which should startle him and make him ready for going hence. But my prudence and calculation to do about right, and my sincerity and my general good intent, did not hinder me from being left.

And if it had been heaven I was going to, instead of Ashland, I should have missed it, in spite of my sincerity and blundering good intention.

Now I knew that I had another chance, like a man calculating on a future hour for salvation. And the knowledge that I had this chance had made me easy about losing the first. I did not care much about the first anyway. There was a freight train half an hour later; and I had once seen what I sincerely supposed was this train spinning through Framingham at great speed with two cars, only a little later than the regular passenger; and I argued from this isolated fact that perhaps going by freight would not be very bad after all. So many another man, with very slight knowledge of spiritual things, concludes to risk having good luck on the next chance. I was sincere in the belief that I should get to South Framingham by supper-time, but I was three hours and a half on the road, and should have partially perished, had it not been for a cracker man and milk woman who pitied me, as I, half famished, hung round the lonely freight houses on that railroad, looking wistfully for a little salt-fish.

It was my purpose to walk or ride from South Framingham a mile and a half to Deacon Thompson's, to find lodging; but when I arrived at the end of my freighting, at quarter of ten, I saw standing behind another freight on the Worcester road the toplights of a passenger train. Here it was that my sincerity helped me. I was a sincere believer in the dogma that an accommodation train from Boston reaches Ashland at about half-past nine P. M. This doctrine I had imbibed by a consultation of railroad documents about three months before, when I was first discussing the great question how to get to Ashland. I am confident that my study of this subject was as thorough as that which many persons give to the great question, how late they can start for heaven. This sincere belief of mine had been lying dormant for all these weeks. It was now to become a power in my life. I concluded, as soon as I saw that long row of lights, that this must be the accommodation between Boston and Ashland, rather late. This I determined to take, and put up at the Ashland or Central House, rather than bother Brother Thompson at a late hour.

This purpose was based on my fundamental principles to act on my sincere beliefs and do about as well as I can, running the risk that all will come out about right. And my prudence also put in its appearance when I was creeping under the freight train, which stood between me and my accommodation train. This I did at the suggestion of the very obliging Framingham conductor, who waited upon me with his lantern, assuring me that the Worcester would not start and smash my tall hat or my head. The view I had entertained on the subject of that train since my profound investigation of the topic three months before, was now confirmed by the impression I received from this affable conductor. Was he not a railroad man? It seemed to me likely that he must know about all railways, and certainly this train I was after; and it was by his shining light that I took the journey under the cars, which under any other guidance I should have thought rather risky. He guided me on the way, and warned me not. Suppose now he had called himself a " Liberal Christian " minister, and had said to me :

" Just go ahead. It is no matter what you believe if you are only sincere. If you do about right, I guess you'll come out about right. Your motive is good ; you are going to preach. And you have been painstaking on my freight ; now only be prudent in getting between these wheels and you will be all right. A man who believes that that train is an accommodation so sincerely as you do, can make no serious mistake in taking it. You can't expect to do just right always ; go on then and do *about* right, and you'll come out *about* right."

" That is where you are right, Mr. Liberal Conductor," I imagine myself replying in the light of experience; " that is exactly so."

I asked a man at the station whether this was the Western accommodation, and received an affirmative answer. He was as smooth and conciliating, and as willing to foster in me my sincere belief, as if he had been a Universalist clergyman. He seemed to have no hesitation whatever in encouraging me to risk all on that train to Ashland. I saw the conductor of that train; it was not, however, convenient to get at him amid a crowd of men tinkering the engine. But it seemed to me that his face was familiar; I had undoubtedly seen him on one of the many accommodations of that very accommodating road. There was no ticket agent up at that time of night, and nobody else I could consult. I was prudent, and I would have asked several more people whether I was right, if I had seen anybody who knew more than I did about that train. I entered a car, and found about twenty students, four at least more or less under the influence of liquor. I gave the conductor ten cents at just about the time I was whizzing by Deacon Thompson's house within three rods of it. He did not appear willing to take it. Did not know what I meant. This was an express for New York, and *would not stop* for *twenty-three miles.* Would not stop that train for his own father to get off to preach in Ashland. He must take up a contribution on me for sixty-five cents. And so I went to Worcester. Those drunken college boys were just as sincere as I was, believing that they were on the road to happiness; and in their way they did about right, not getting *very* drunk; and they were prudent, not allowing the drunkest ones to go out on the platform; and their designs were good; they were to keep Sunday in Worcester, or on the Lake, after their fashion. But if they keep on the kind of "train" they were going on then, they will land in perdition as certainly as I landed in Worcester. And their sincerity and aiming to do *about* right, and prudence and meaning well, will not keep them from the remorseless working of spiritual laws, any more than mine saved me from that unpitying express train.

The Waverly House clerk said the cook would rap at my door at four in the morning, so I could take the early express back to South Framingham, whence I could aim once more for my pulpit. But if I had laid abed till he called me, perhaps I should have been there now, and you never would have received this article. But I took the business into my own hands of getting up and being off in time, and you have this article.

ONLY A JOKE.

WAS always fond of a joke," said Uncle Moses Fuller to the friends who had assembled to commemorate the golden wedding of his good wife, Aunt Patty, and himself. " But jokes have their proper times and places, and that reminds me of a little story that I will relate to you, young people, while mother is in the other room taking down the old china.

" Some of you are married now, and some of you are likely to be at no distant day — if there is any truth in signs or in hearsay — and none of you will object to receiving a mild lesson from an old man.

" I was always fond of a ' joke,' as I was saying, but I never 'joked' my wife but once. That was after we had been married about a week, and had got nicely to housekeeping. The old minister who had married us, and who had known us both all our lives, and his wife, came to make us a call, and Patty urged them to stay to tea. They accepted the invitation so cordially given with evident pleasure.

" As they were our first visitors, Patty wanted to put her best foot forward, of course; so she made hot biscuit for supper. I remember as if it were only yesterday, how pretty she looked in her blue home-made gown, and clean, freshly-starched check apron, as she was stepping around in her shy, quiet, womanly way, making the biscuit, looking at and turning them in the tin baker before the open fire-place, setting the table, and pleasantly talking with her guests at the same time; for we had no parlor then.

"I felt quite proud of her, I assure you, when we drew our chairs around the neatly spread and bountifully loaded table, and just at that moment I thought more, I fear, of Parson and Mrs. Bancroft's opinion of Patty's cooking and housekeeping than I did of the grace he was saying. Both of our guests praised the light, short, properly browned biscuit, and Patty's girlish face flushed with genuine pleasure as she shyly glanced up at my face for her husband's approval.

"But I did not speak, and presently she asked timidly: 'I hope you like them, Moses, for they are the first biscuit I have made since — since —' 'Since you became Mrs. Fuller,' said the parson's wife, considerately helping out her speech.

"'Oh, yes,' I replied flippantly, thinking it would not do to praise my wife before company, and not relishing the possibility of losing an opportunity to get off one of my 'jokes.' 'I like them, to be sure; but I should hate to have anybody throw one of them at my head, for the consequences might be serious.' Patty's countenance changed as if she had received a blow, and wife-like she tried to throw off her ill concealed mortification at my thoughtless speech. Although I could find no fault with the way she performed her duties as hostess, I noticed she ate very little of the supper.

"Mr. and Mrs. Bancroft started for their home just before dark, and as I was tucking them up in their comfortable old chaise I thought what a happy, contented old couple they were. When I handed the parson the reins, after everything was ready, and they had bidden Patty 'good-night,' and she had gone back through the gate into the yard, he leaned down toward me, and putting his trembling hand on my shoulder, said : 'My son, bear in mind that pure, burnished gold even may be scratched and defaced by rough usage.'

"I felt like a brute all the time I was getting the cows, and milking and doing the chores. When I carried into the kitchen the brimming pails of milk, Patty was washing and polishing and putting away that very china she is now taking down, and I could see in the gathering twilight that she had been crying. I kissed her impulsively with my heart in my throat, and catching the empty water-pail started for the well. I didn't make any promises to anybody but to myself.

"The moon was shining high in the heavens, and as I ran down the bucket I saw it reflected in the clear water at the bottom of the round, deep well. I felt as if it might be Patty's love going down, down, far beyond my reach, slipping away from me forever. As I drew up the brimming, mossy bucket, the brilliant harvest moon was reflected upon that, too, in broken flashes of light, shining up curiously from the dark depths of the well. I hurriedly drew up the smooth pole, feeling that I was regaining what I had come near losing.

"I set the overflowing bucket down upon the soft, green grass, and let it be until the perturbed water became still and smooth like a mirror. Then looking into it I saw the moon peaceful and calm once more. I emptied the bucket into my pail, and as I did so, I said aloud: 'I will never joke Patty again. She is gentle and sweet, and sensitive; far too good for a rough fellow like me. I will never grieve her tender, loving heart by my peculiar kind of joking again.'

"And I have kept my word. We were married fifty years ago to-day, and although I have had my jokes with other people — jokes that they say are 'rather cutting, though Uncle Moses don't mean anything' — I have never joked my wife. She has proved to be unalloyed gold, and, thanks to the good old parson's advice, it has not been defaced or had its luster dimmed by rough usage. I have never happened to see the moon reflected in the old well without the memory of those supremely unhappy moments coming back to me. Life is short at the best, young people, and you cannot be too careful about wounding the sensibilities of those who are nearest and dearest to you."

UNDER THE LILIES.

THIS casket with choice lilies spread,
Contains a mortal doubly dead —
He died in the esteem of men,
And yesterday he died again.

O, lightly hold thy gold and gem !
Some one at last will care for them;
But keep thy fame in thine own trust,
And with thy deeds perfume thy dust.

MR. FINNEY IN A MOMENT OF PERIL.

HE revival of religion in western New York, in the year 1826, created a profound impression all over the land. Mr. Finney's preaching was attended with most remarkable effects. His leading topics were: The sovereignty and holiness of God; the rebellion of the sinner; the perfect equity of the divine law, its absolute necessity for the safety of the moral universe, and the entire obligation of every man to obey it perfectly.

The scene of our narrative was in the city of Troy, New York. Dr. N. S. S. Beaman was pastor of the First Presbyterian Church, which was large and influential, and, as is well known, Dr. Beaman was a popular and effective preacher. He invited Mr. Finney to labor with him in Troy. Many were opposed to him, and Mr. Finney reluctantly consented. The same effects which were produced in Oneida county were soon visible in Troy. Mr. Finney's preaching was exceedingly powerful, and numbers were hopefully converted. Every prop of self-righteousness was swiftly, and sometimes rudely, swept away, and it may be doubted whether the intense feeling that prevailed did not betray these excellent men into some measures that were neither warrantable nor wise. Opposition in a violent form was soon developed; a portion of the members of the church protested in a published pamphlet against the action of the pastor and Mr. Finney. Nevertheless the work of conversion went on with remarkable power, and men of leading positions in society could not resist the force of truth, and became humble followers of Christ, and this feature of deep humility and self-abasement was strikingly developed in the experience of those who were hopefully converted.

It happened in the midst of this excitement that Mr. Finney preached to an overflowing assembly from the words in Isaiah xxviii: 22: " Now, therefore, be ye not mockers, lest your bands be made strong," etc. It was a sermon of immense power. It arraigned the professed Christian, and summoned him to deep repentance for his backwardness in the work of revival, pointed out the various ways in which Christians mocked God, and reproved them with marked severity; and then, passing to the unconverted, he pictured their guilt and danger in most appalling colors, and swept away every refuge of lies. The sermon excited the most angry feelings on every side. Many were perfectly enraged, and declared that if Mr. Finney dared to preach such a sermon again, they would club him in the pulpit, and drive him out of the church. They endeavored to put a stop to his preaching, but Dr. Beaman, and a majority of the church, insisted that under his ministry so many were converted, they dared not oppose the manifest work of God; and, moreover, it was nothing but the nakedness and power of truth, which, while it developed this intense hostility in some minds, was, in fact, turning multitudes from the error of their ways to the love and service of God.

In the midst of all this, Mr. Finney was calm and undismayed. He trusted in God that He would deliver him from the power of these wicked men, and enable him to deliver his message with all boldness and fidelity. It was announced that he would preach again, and his exasperated enemies publicly declared that they would go to church with canes and clubs in their hands, and chastise him on the spot, if he dared to repeat the sentiments of his former sermon. It was expected that some angry demonstration would take place, and the church was thronged in every part. This expectation was increased when Mr. Finney announced his text: " The carnal mind is enmity against God : for it is not subject to the law of God, neither indeed can be." Not in the least did this fearless, devoted man disguise or soften the truths he was called to utter. He may not have been wise, and was often mistaken in some views of duty, but no one doubted his entire earnestness and sincerity. For a time there was silence in the church, and Mr.

Finney proceeded unmolested with his solemn subject; but in the utterance of one of his naked truths, a low murmur was heard, which soon rose to a menacing distinctness. Mr. Finney, however, did not allow himself to be interrupted, but proceeded with his sermon. Louder and louder came the angry demonstration from all parts of the church, until the agitation of the audience became extreme, and the voice of Mr. Finney could no longer be heard. He therefore paused, standing erect in the pulpit, and looking undismayed upon the turbulent elements around him. Apparently anxious to know what he would do next, and expecting he would apologize, the noisy element was for a moment suppressed ; a perfect stillness reigned through the church. At this moment, in a deeply subdued and solemn tone, Mr. Finney uttered the following words :

"I learn that some of you have come this evening to the house of God, to inflict what you suppose merited punishment on me; but oh, my friends, what _profit is there in my blood? will it plead for you at the bar of God? Rather reserve all your strength for your last dreadful conflict with your last enemy. Take those clubs and beat off death! beat off death! This were a higher wisdom than to strike down a poor mortal like me."

Opposition and violence were now at an end. The services proceeded to their close uninterrupted save by the suppressed sigh of the penitent and the sometimes audible sob of the broken-hearted.

The foregoing incidents were related to me for substance by one of the friends of Mr. Finney. Perhaps I am not accurate in all the details, as I have to rely on my memory; but in the main I am confident of their truth. We need not justify Mr. Finney in all things; we cannot do it; but that he was a chosen instrument of vast good to the church, and a man eminently gifted for his great work, cannot be denied. George Whitefield and Rowland Hill were both eccentric, but they were eminent blessings to the church and the world.

ANSWERING A FOOL ACCORDING TO HIS FOLLY.

"Answer not a fool according to his folly, lest thou be like unto him.

"Answer a fool according to his folly, lest he be wise in his own conceit." — *Proverbs, xxvi: 4, 5.*

E are here directed *not* to answer a fool according to his folly, and *to answer* him according to his folly, an apparent contradiction, but certainly not a real one. The Wise Man would never have uttered a real, intentional contradiction, within the compass of two contiguous verses. To do so would have proved himself a fool.

The ambiguity in these verses lies in the connecting words, *according to*, which are here used in two different senses. " Answer not a fool according to his folly," *i. e.*, not in a manner *according with* his folly, or *agreeing with it*, lest thou become as foolish and perverse as he. " Answer a fool according to his folly," *i. e.*, according to *the nature and desert of his folly* — so as best to meet and refute it — to silence him and prevent harm to others;

"lest he be wise in his own conceit." We have many examples in the Scriptures, and in common life, going to illustrate the wisdom of this second direction of Solomon. The following one was given me many years ago by a venerable minister now deceased. I have reason to suppose it genuine, though I have not inquired particularly about it; since, whether the fact took place as related or not, the example is equally apposite and instructive.

About a hundred years ago the Rev. John Murray, the father of modern Universalism, performed a preaching tour through the country. He preached, among other places at New Haven, Connecticut, where he had for a hearer Dr. Edwards, son of the first President Edwards. Mr. Murray preached on the *paternal character of God*, representing Him as the universal Father, and setting forth His great love for His children, and for all His children. The preacher closed with a very earnest appeal to his audience against the doctrine of eternal punishment.

" Would any of you who are parents plunge your children into everlasting fire, and hold them there in torment forever? And does not God love His children as well as you love yours? And can you believe that He will cast off any of His children, and punish them in hell to all eternity? Impossible! The thought is too dreadful to be endured!" The sermon was artfully drawn up, and eloquently closed, and was evidently making quite an impression.

When the services were over and before any of the people had left the house, Dr. Edwards rose in his place, and asked permission to append a few remarks. "You have heard," said he, "of the paternal character of God, and the inference has been drawn, from His great love for His creatures, that He will not punish any of them forever in the future world.

"Now, it does not seem to me that the preacher has drawn out inferences enough from this doctrine. He should have drawn more, and with your permission, and his, I will assist him in his conclusions. Would any of you who are parents, cast your children into the sea, or dart them upon the rocks and cause them to be drowned and perish? Impossible! You could not do it! And does not God love His children as well as you love yours? And do you believe that He will ever suffer any of them to be drowned in the sea? Assuredly not. Nobody ever was drowned in the sea, or ever can be, under the government of God.

"Again, would any of you who are parents throw your beloved children into the fire to be tortured and consumed? Would you set fire to your dwellings in the night, and cause your sleeping, unconscious babe to be burned to death? Impossible! You could not do it! And does not God love His children as well as you love yours? And do you believe that He will ever suffer a fire to be kindled upon any of them to consume them? No such thing! No one ever was consumed in a burning house, or ever will be. To suppose such a thing would be a reflection on the paternal character of God.

"Still again; would any of you who are parents visit your dear children with sore and mortal sickness, and see them languish from day to day, and then see them pass away in the agonies of death, when you could save them at any time with a word? Impossible! You could not do it! And does not God love His children as well as you love yours? And do you think that He will inflict sickness and pain, and agonies, and death, upon any of His children, which you would not inflict upon yours? No, my friends, never! *never!* According to the argument to which you have listened, no one ever was sick, or suffered pain, or died, under the government of God, or ever will."

Dr. Edwards was about to introduce some further inferences, but Mr. Murray could stand it no longer. He caught his hat and left the house, and the assembly was broken up. The fool had been answered according to his folly. The sermon was spoiled. It was evident to every one, that if the argument of the preacher proved anything, it proved vastly too much. It contradicted the plainest facts, and consequently was good for nothing.

WHAT PINKIE-BLUE DON'T KNOW.

My Pinkie-Blue is as fair as a rose,
But as yet of this not a lisp she knows,
    And I wouldn't have her know;
If she knew she might prink and put on airs
And go thinking about the clothes she wears —
    So I wouldn't have her know.

Pinkie-Blue wears silk, but, then, she don't know
That it's any better than calico,
    And I wouldn't have her know;
For, when she begins to turn up her nose,
No longer she'll be as sweet as a rose —
    So I wouldn't have her know.

But now, with the washerwoman's baby all day
Pinkie-Blue will merrily, sweetly play,
    And I wouldn't have her know
Any one could think the play wasn't right,
Or the black skin not as good as the white —
    No, I wouldn't have her know.

A smile is a smile with my Pinkie-Blue,
She believes that smiles are as true as true,
    And I wouldn't have her know
That a smile may tell the naughtiest lies
And sweet looks say what the heart denies —
    No, I wouldn't have her know.

THE RUSSIAN NIHILISTS.

HE main difference between the Russian Nihilists and the German and French Socialists, is that, while the Socialists have a vague programme of government to set up in place of that they propose to pull down, the Nihilists hold a creed of destruction, pure and simple. The Russian Nihilists believe, as their name implies, simply in nothing. They seek to destroy; the building up that is to come after they leave to the future. They are atheists, iconoclasts; they would destroy the State, and, equally, the church. Never was fanaticism carried to a more dreary, chaotic extreme. One would think their ideas the chimeras of insanity. Yet it is not true, as the Russian government, contemptuous of truth in the very hour of dire perils, would have the world believe, that the Nihilists are small in number and feeble in power, though malignant in act and purpose. We know on pretty good authority, that these followers of "King Anarch" in Russia are to be counted literally by millions. There are sixty thousand destructive Socialists in Berlin alone; and not fewer Nihilists in St. Petersburg. I have seen one statement that there are three millions in all Russia.

But the importance of the Nihilists is not to be reckoned by numbers alone. Consider the classes from which these numbers are recruited. Not long ago, the daughter of a noble lady who belongs to the household of one of the Grand Duchesses, was arrested as a Nihilist. It is perfectly well known that the Nihilists include in their number nobles of the highest rank, generals of long service, women of gentle blood, lofty social position and great wealth, chiefs of police, priests of the national church, famous lawyers and doctors, university professors, great landed proprietors, and, it is more than suspected, trusted officials of the administration, and even governors of provinces. Nay, the taint of suspicion attaches even to the heir to the throne himself. The statement has been reiterated that the Czarowitz is a Nihilist. When Vera. Sassulitch, a highly educated young woman and a Nihilist, shot the chief of St. Petersburg police, General Trepoff, in his office, she was tried by a jury, half of whom were officials of the Imperial administration; *yet she was acquitted.* It is but a year or two since seventy gentlemen and ladies of social rank, some of ducal and princely rank, were seized one night at the capital, hurried away to secret trials, and not seen again. They were charged with socialistic sedition, and were sent to Siberia.

It is scarcely a year since the strange fact was discovered, that " in Switzerland there existed a society of more than two hundred Russian female students, ardently devoted and giving all their time and energies to the cause of revolution." When we descend in the social strata, we find merchants, commercial travelers, students, petty tradespeople, in the ranks of Nihilism, swearing self-abnegation and even self-immolation in the cause, and unquestioningly obeying the orders of a secret committee, whose very names and locality are unknown to them. Nihilism, it is very moderate to say, counts peasants and small landed proprietors by the thousand. There are probably few Russian villages where there is not hid the cocoon of a conspiracy. –

A great element in the now evident and terrible power of Nihilism lies in the consummate craft with which it is organized, governed and directed. Its mystery of organization is enough to make the timid and hypochondriacal Czar quake with fear. Its central committee has absolute power, is completely hid from view, even from its own members; the other committees, scattered in a network throughout the length and breadth of that vast empire, are equally secret in locality and operation. They send out their orders, and the rank and file obey. Men are designated to the grim task of assassination ; and they go forth and assassinate, if they can — with the stoicism of martyrs to a sacred cause. The man who shot at the Czar confessed that he had been chosen to do this by lot, and by order of a secret committee.

It is not too much to say that hundreds of Nihilists are already expiating their seditious plotting in the dreary wastes of Siberia. There must now, in all probability, be a yet greater holocaust of victims. So overcome by terror is the government, that the six largest cities in Russia — St. Petersburg, Moscow, Warsaw, Odessa, Charkoff, and Kieff — are handed over to the mercies of military governors, armed with the barbaric powers of an Asiatic despotism. These governors may arrest, imprison, execute, any man, woman, or child, within their districts, without trial, without notice, with not a moment's delay for defense or disproof.

We may well wonder, however, whether it never occurs to Russian statesmen to consider seriously the *causes* of Nihilism, and to attack the evil at the root. Siamese tyranny and cruelty will only aggravate it in the end. Persecution and despotism are, indeed, the very food upon which it thrives. It is the persecution, the oppression of the past, that has given it being, upon which it has been nourished and has grown. It is almost enough to account for Nihilism, to say that Russia is the only government in Europe in which the people have no part. Sooner or later the autocrat must grant a constitution, or he and his house, and his swarms of corrupt officials, and his elaborate system of almost Tartaric despotism, are doomed. The people are beginning to find out their power; and when that period comes in the life of a nation, it is time for despots to bend or be broken.

IN ME, O LORD, ABIDE.

In me, O Lord, abide,
  And I in Thee !
No more let sin divide ;
  'Tis love's decree.
Uncertain all my skill:
Work out Thy holy will:
  In me, O Lord, abide,
    And I in Thee.

Thus, o'er and o'er I pray,
  In me abide.
Teach me Thy perfect way:
  Walk by my side.
Thine are life's precious hours :
Thine all my ransomed powers :
  In me, O Lord, abide,
    And I in Thee.

In me, O Lord, abide !
  Give daily grace.
Be still Thy wounded side
  My hiding place.
Thou art mine only One !
Give me the secret stone.
  In me, O Lord, abide,
    And I in Thee.

MAN PROPOSES, BUT GOD DISPOSES.

HIRTY-SEVEN years ago the eleventh day of March, 1878, the steamer President lay in New York harbor ready to start for Liverpool. Right beside it lay a sailing vessel, the Sir Isaac Newton, also on the point of leaving, bound for Germany. A foreign gentleman and his family, who were going home to Hamburg, had engaged their passage on the sailing vessel, and their baggage was already on board. When, however, the family came on board, the gentleman noticed with surprise a large engine strapped upon the deck. It was a locomotive being sent to Austria, as the United States at that time supplied that country with many railroad engines; and this one proving too large for the hold had been secured on deck.

"I do not like the looks of that engine," said the foreigner, uneasily. "In case of a storm it might be loosened from its position and make trouble aboard."

There was but a moment to decide. He looked at the President, a large, fine-looking steamer, and made up his mind to embark upon her. Instantly he gave orders for the transfer of his baggage, which was no sooner accomplished than the President was freed from her moorings, and, with a feeling of relief in having secured the change, he and his family gladly turned their faces homeward. No whispered oracle told of the coming doom. Just when the vessel yielded to the power of the terrific storm which two days later it encountered; whether suddenly or with prolonged agony its many passengers met their awful fate, no one was saved to tell. The vessel *started.* It never reached the destined shore. Between those two facts its terrible secret lies hidden until the day when "the sea shall give up its dead." The friend who recently told me this incident embarked on the sailing vessel, which left at the same hour as the President, encountered the same storm, but reached its destination in safety.

There are mysteries in life which it is in vain for us to attempt to explain. We call them providences, and we well may, for they are certainly not the work of man. We plan and act for what seems our best good, and the result proves the exact opposite of our intentions. It may be to our destruction; it may be to our salvation. Instances similar to this may come to the recollection of many who read it. I once stood with a mother as she bent in agony over the grave of her first-born son, with a grief which found vent in the reiterated expression of her one thought: "I did it!" He was about leaving her after a vacation spent at home, and after the good-by was said, she followed him to the gate, and in the sorrow at parting, begged him to remain "one day longer." Although disturbing his plans, he yielded, stayed the one day longer, and left her the next morning to meet his fate before the sunset — one among many victims of a fearful railroad disaster.

One other incident will never be forgotten. I was spending an evening many years since with a party of young people, when, in the midst of a game, the hilarity was hushed by the announcement: "The Monongahela has sunk." Many a face turned pale, and hurrying home some spent the night in bitter weeping. A party of friends, some of them brothers and sisters, had written that they would return on that boat, and were expected the next day.

In this case the sorrow was turned into joy. The friends came home safely, and the singular explanation followed: "Our trunks were put on board the Monongahela, and we had no other thought than to return by that boat, when some one of the party, almost thoughtlessly, proposed spending a day longer in P—. After a little talking and laughing over it, this was decided on, the baggage was taken off, and the party saved. God, after all, is in the decision. Man proposes, but He disposes."

While we may tremble to take any such responsibility into our own hands, if we "commit our way unto Him," we shall be led aright. It is a fearful thing to venture alone upon the great sea before us all; but here we may be *sure* of being brought into a safe haven. If God is our guide, even a wreck like that of the President will but bring us into *this* port in safety.

"What harm," said Archbishop Leighton, after having been barely saved from drowning in a boat on his way to Lambeth, when spoken to by a fellow-passenger on being so calm during the danger, "what harm would it have been if we had all been safe landed on *the other side?*" This faith is the "anchor" which "entereth in to that within the vail."

THE STRANGER'S TESTIMONY.

FAR down on the coast of Maine the bell of the village church was ringing for prayer-meeting. It reached the ears of Frank, the lighthouse-keeper's son, as, aloft in the tower, he helped his father about their evening duties.

"There's the old bell," said the elder; "I'll bide at home to-night, lad; do you go ashore to the meeting."

So it happened that Frank went that Sabbath evening. It was a pleasant change to row across the water in the sunset, and join the young men in the back seat of the ancient church. He did not expect to be interested, however; he thought old "Parson Porter" dull, and the brethren were not gifted with eloquent speech. Frank fancied they said about the same thing every time, often wondering if their remarks had originally been committed to memory. The truth was, pastor and people needed to be roused; they had fallen into listless formality. But on the whole, there was to Frank something attractive in the place of prayer — an indefinable presence that made him thoughtful and reverent, and increased that vague yearning after something better that fills every fresh young heart. For Frank, while helping his father in their fortress-like home in the waters, had been kept singularly free from evil companions, had grown to vigorous manhood, one thing only lacking — faith in Christ.

The stillness was broken at length by the pastor, who read the Scripture selection; prayer was offered, a hymn sung, and the meeting was "in the hands of the brethren." This announcement was followed by deep silence. Apparently the brethren had nothing to say, or modestly waited for each other. At last the senior deacon offered a labored prayer. Then there was another pause. It seemed a little ludicrous to the young lookers-on in the rear, who exchanged amused glances. Frank, also, felt disposed to smile at the reluctant laymen.

"If I were a Christian, I'd find something to say!" he thought.

At this juncture a stranger rose, a weather-beaten, broad-shouldered son of the sea. There was an earnest, decided air in his quick uprising that roused all present like an electric thrill.

"My friends," said he, "I stand before you to-night as a stranger. But I trust I am not a stranger to Jesus Christ, in whose house we are met to pray and praise. I have tried to serve Him for five years. His word and service grow more precious each day. Wherever I am, I give my testimony for Jesus. It's humble enough, but He has

said : 'Ye are my witnesses,' and all who overcome
do so by the blood of the Lamb and the word of
their testimony. I trust He will bless my words to
some sin-laden soul here. I came into your little
harbor with the morning tide. I go out with the
next tide. Probably you will never see me again.
If there is one in this room who does not love my
Master, let me beseech you to delay no longer.
You are drifting upon the rocks; take warning
from your chart, the Bible; that beacon light to
guide you into a safe port. The 'still small voice'
of God's spirit is speaking to some heart in this
room ; are you trying to hush its pleadings ?" His
keen eyes searched each face a moment, and it
seemed to Frank that they lingered on him. Suddenly the stillness grew awful, as he thought that
perhaps the pleading voice of the Spirit was speaking to him! The stranger then recited, with deep
emotion : "My Spirit shall not always strive with
man ;" and for the first time there came to Frank
an overwhelming sense of what it was to resist conviction. "You hear this knocking at the door of
your heart," the stranger went on; "it is Jesus
standing without, the print of the nails on His
sacred hands and feet — the great Creator and
Redeemer, who stooped to suffer for your sins
and mine. Oh, will you not hear His voice, and
open the door that He may bless and save you ?"

It was something new, this fervent yet simple
appeal. It wondrously loosened the tongues of the

brethren, for they spoke and prayed as never before — short, pithy, fervent. The old pastor's voice faltered as he closed the meeting by thanking God for the blessed hour they had spent in His house. As for Frank, he rushed out as soon as possible, and, without exchanging a word with his comrades, hastened to the shore, unmoored his boat, and was soon rowing swiftly through the waves. He was like one fleeing from a pursuing foe; but it was of no avail. Leaving the church behind did not help him forget the stranger's appeal. The arrow of conviction had entered his soul. He would find no healing for the wound till he surrendered his will to Christ. As he crossed the bay he passed the schooner that had brought the stranger, and between him and the shore he could descry a skiff approaching, which doubtless held the stranger returning from the meeting.

"If he'd kept still I'd be happier," muttered Frank. "I wanted to put off being a Christian a few years, but he's stirred me all up!"

The light streaming from the tower amid the waves reminded him that the speaker had likened it to the Bible as a guide to mariners. "I will read and see for myself," he thought; hoping by this good resolve to quiet his awakened conscience. He reached the lighthouse at ebb tide, and the steps to the landing were uncovered. Mounting these, he hauled up his boat, and appeared before his father with such an unhappy face that the old man exclaimed:

"Why, lad, you don't look so peart as you did when you started for the shore; what's befallen ye?"

Frank did not open his heart to his father, but sat beside him in silence till he retired, dreading to be left alone with his convictions. That night was one never to be forgotten by him. The "still small voice" spoke in tones that would not be stifled. At last the young man surrendered himself to Christ, and found peace. So great was his happiness that he could not rest until he had told some one. He sought his father at midnight with shining face and eager voice, to tell him that he had found the Saviour.

"I wanted to begin giving my testimony," said Frank, "as the good man did from yonder schooner — I mean to rise up very early to-morrow and thank him for it!"

"It wasn't my testimony that set you in the right track," said the old lighthouse-keeper with emotion; "but I'm glad ye've started, lad; I'll help ye in my poor way!"

Morning had scarcely tinted the gray stone of the lighthouse, when Frank ascended to the top to look for the stranger's ship. It was not in sight. He searched the ocean far and wide with his father's glass, but not a sail was in sight. The stranger had left as quietly as he came. He had told the story of the cross, risen up before day and gone on his way. But his "testimony" bore precious fruit, for several of Frank's comrades also found peace in believing. And after that, many other hearts were opened to receive the Master.

The stranger has never since appeared in the little seaport, and perhaps his voice is silenced for earthly testimony ; but he is not forgotten. Frank never enters the boat to answer the summons to Sabbath worship or evening prayer, but his eye wistfully searches the water for the stranger whose earnest words became, through God, such a blessing.

EXPERIENCES WITH TRAMPS.

S it well to give to beggars at the door? That was the question we had been discussing one day in the seminary. My own answer was: "I don't believe it is wise stewardship of God's money, and I will not do it." Some thought the position wrong; that it would be cruel, *un-Christian* not to help a person whose story of want seemed to be honest.

That afternoon the door-bell rang, and, the janitor being out, I answered the call. A very pleasant lady stood before me, neatly attired, dignified, and with prepossessing face.

"Will you please give me enough to buy a loaf of bread?"

"No; we have a city missionary whose business is to help such people as you. Go to him, and he will give you all the bread you need."

"Yes, sir; but I have been to him, and he has given me all he has to spare, and there isn't enough for us."

Who could resist such an appeal? I gave her ten cents.

"Please, sir, have you any old clothes that I could cut over for my little boys?"

"I will look, and call on you; where do you live?"

She named the street and number. Saturday afternoon was very stormy, but I determined to test her truthfulness, and to relieve her wants if they existed. For two miles I pushed through sleet and slush, to find *that no person by that name lived on the street.*

One day there called at the parsonage a lady, for so she seemed, who told a very sad story. She had been married but a few years, had two small children, was in poor health, her husband had deserted her; the rent was due, and the landlord had threatened to turn the family into the street. But she had a sister in New Hampshire, like herself very poor, who had promised to give her a home, if they could get together. "Will you give me something toward paying my fare?"

I replied: "We have a society of ladies, who make it their business to inquire into such cases. I will write a note in your behalf and send by you to them." I put her story on paper, asked an examination of the case, sealed, and directed it to the president. The lady left me with many thanks. *But that note never was presented.*

"O dear, I must work on my sermon," said I to the girl who knocked to say that a man at the door wanted to see me.

"Good morning, sir."

"Good morning!"

"Is this Brother Makepeace of the Orthodox church ?"

"This is *Mr.* Makepeace," I replied.

"Well now, brother, I ain't a Orthodox. I belong to the Baptists; but it's all the same, you know — 'one Lord, one faith, and one baptism.' I come down from Portsmouth to git work, but I can't git any, and I'm going back. I'm willing to walk, cuz p'raps I can git work on the way, but I hate to go lookin' so, and come to see if you wouldn't give me a clean shirt."

Being refused, he went directly to one of the deacons, as I sometime afterward learned, and said:

"Your pastor told me you was a large-hearted man, and you'd help a feller; now won't you give me a little money to help me toward Portsmouth ?"

Being again refused, he went to the Methodist pastor and asked for work. The pastor sent him to a business man of his society, who judged the fellow to be a "fraud," and dismissed him. But he at once went back to the pastor, and said:

"Mr. P——, that you sent me to, gave me this dollar, and now if you'll give me one more, it'll be all I need."

The money was given.

A few days after these occurrences, a letter came to me from the pastor of a neighboring church, and this was followed by other letters, all telling the same story, saying that a member of my church had called, in distress, and asking the loan of a few dollars, with which to reach home. He was foot-sore and very tired. His mother was a widow, living on the same street with me, and at such a number. The money had been loaned, but not returned, as promised. Had this poor brother reached home? It is, perhaps, needless to add that the fellow hadn't arrived, that there was no person of the name given in my church, and that the houses of our street had not been numbered. I had to advertise the wretch, my only comfort being found in his voluntary confession that he " ain't a Orthodox."

On going down to dinner one day, the deacon with whom I was boarding at the time, introduced me to Mr. ——. I forget his name. He had pre-viously met my host, and said to him : "I am grad-uated from —— college (somewhere in the Prov-inces), and while studying incurred a debt, which now I am trying to pay. In the fall I am to enter a theological seminary. I came to town a few weeks since to canvass for a book ; had very good success, and have now returned to deliver them. But the books which I had ordered to be sent here have not arrived. As I brought no money, I am in trouble. Will you loan me two dollars?"

My friend offered him more than he asked. At table I met him, supposed him to be a friend of the family, and was happy to give him the information he wanted about various seminaries. He inquired after several professors *by name*, showing himself to be no novice. On entering my study, he picked up my Tischendorf, and translated off-hand part of the Latin introduction. He left his address. The name I forget; the town was Fitchburg, Mass. But we searched earnestly, "*and he was not, for the devil had taken him.*" *Neither did his books arrive.*

To decide rightly between cases of misery true and fabricated, is not an easy matter, especially where there are neither city missionaries nor boards of relief to examine into them. Among the methods of detection, none perhaps is better than to ask fictitious questions. As a good illustration of this, I will give the experience of a ministerial friend. During the early part of the war, a young negro called upon him, asking money by which to buy the liberty of his mother and sister, who were still in slavery.

"Where did you say you used to live?"

"In Richmond, sah."

"O, indeed; then you knew General Buell, of course?"

"O yes, sah. I work for him long time."

"Then you have seen that splendid span of black horses?"

"Yes, sah; I dribe um eb'ry day."

"Where does the General buy his meat now?"

He gave the market.

"Then you must remember old Tommy the butcher?"

" O yes; see him many a time."

" By the way, that was a queer idea of the general, about his doors — they were all oval, weren't they ? "

" Yes, sah."

" Didn't it trouble you to get through the doors ? "

" No, sah. I used to put de sarber on my head and den walk up de little steps, fro de door, and down on de ubber side."

" Yes ; well, there were no stairs in that house ? "

" No, sah."

" The family slept up stairs ? "

" Yes, sah."

" Well, how did they get up to the chambers."

" O, dey pull dem-sells up on de rope."

" Well, whatever money I have to give to you, I'll send down to New Haven."

A few years later, my friend was attending worship in S——, when the Rev. Dr. B—— arose and said : " A colored brother has called on me during the past week, and profoundly interested me in his behalf. He desires to obtain sufficient money to send his mother and sister to Liberia. I did not see fit to ask a general collection in his behalf, but, at my request, he will take his stand at —— gate, on —— Avenue, to receive whatever you may be disposed to give, and as Ethiopia shall stretch out her hands, I hope that you will make a liberal response."

My friend believed that his old acquaintance had

arrived, and sent a note to the desk stating his suspicions. The assisting clergyman read, folded and laid aside the note to give Dr. B—— at the close of service. On seeing this, my friend quietly left the church, went to the gate mentioned, found the rogue as he expected, and saying: "Come here, come here, come round to this gate — quick," he led him to a rear gate, on another avenue. Meanwhile the audience flowed forth, looking in vain for "Ethiopia." My friend then found the Doctor, who was introduced to the "colored brother," and convinced of his villainy.

But recently, this fellow was arrested in Montreal, on the charge of larceny. For nearly a score of years he had lived by deceiving good men.

RECOLLECTIONS OF DR. KIRK.

IT was in New York City in the winter of 1839–40, when I was in the Union Theological Seminary. He came there to labor as an evangelist. That class of ministers was then in disfavor. Nettleton had been laid aside by ill-health, Finney had the vague charge of Oberlinism lying at his door, Burchard was said to be flighty, Horatio Foote had gone West, Elder Knapp was called rough and vulgar. Many good men were feeling and saying that the special influences of the Spirit had been withdrawn, and revivals were no longer to be expected. The labors of Kirk in New York that winter proved otherwise, and did much to awaken hope and rekindle the zeal of Christians. They were specially helpful to the young men in the seminary. It was estimated that in connection with his labors and those of Elder Knapp, the Baptist evangelist, there were a thousand conversions in the city.

His manner of preaching was then somewhat novel. He spoke mainly without notes, using only a skeleton, in a simple, direct style, with frequent pithy illustrations, always pertinent, yet never offending a cultivated taste. His voice was melodious, his manner graceful, and, added to all this was an unction and earnestness that at once arrested and moved the hearer. Many of his terse statements and illustrations afterward appeared in the discourses of students who then heard him and unconsciously repeated what had so impressed them. Who can tell how much Moody owes to Kirk, his first pastor? His sentences were short, his words mainly the strong Saxon which everybody understood, and so clearly did his hearers see his ideas that they seldom thought of his words.

Yet one memorable sentence has lingered with me for nearly forty years. He was preaching in the Mercer Street Church, Dr. Skinner's. It was just after the burning of the steamboat Lexington on the Sound, when nearly all the passengers perished; some were burned, some frozen, and some drowned. Only five or six escaped. The event was the sensation of the winter in New York. Mr. Kirk made it preach to the careless and pleasure-loving and mammon-seeking city. Having said that the confidence of skeptics usually forsakes them in near view of death, he exclaimed: "Doubtless, many a scoffer's cry for mercy rent the heavens from the deck of the Lexington, when flame and flood and frost in God's name laid hold of the soul, saying: 'Haste thee away to judgment.'"

I think never in my life did a single sentence so thrill me. Its effect on a crowded sympathizing audience, as uttered by Kirk, may be imagined by those who heard him in his palmiest days, but by scarcely any one else. Could anybody amend and improve it, or change a word without loss of idea or force? I have thought of it a hundred times since, and wondered whether the sentence burst from him spontaneously, or whether he had carefully arranged it in his study.

Take a specimen of his liberal catholic spirit. The famous Elder Knapp, as already said, was in the city at the same time. He was a strong man, a Baptist, and more, a regular John the Baptist, with a burly form, a harsh voice, uncouth, and almost vulgar in his style and illustrations, often disgusting cultured men and women. He was the antipode of Kirk, with his musical voice, graceful manners, and good taste. But Mr. Kirk recognized a fellow-laborer in the other K——, and said to his fastidious audience: "Some of you, to humble your pride, may have to go and hear my dear rough brother Knapp preach, before you can find salvation."

In a familiar talk, before a class of theological students, giving his own experience for their benefit, he said: "My voice was naturally weak. My first attempt at speaking before my fellow-students was a failure. My utterance was so rapid and indistinct that I was laughed off the stage. Excessively mortified, I set myself to learn how to speak. I soon found that some of the sweetest sounds of my

mother tongue I had never made. By diligent practice, by cultivating musical tones, and by distinctness of articulation I have become able, despite my
naturally weak voice, to make myself heard easily
in the largest churches." Yes, even his whispers
could be heard in the remotest part of the house.

Illustrating the value of *distinctness* rather than
loudness, he told this story: A lawyer wished to
destroy the testimony of a deaf witness before a
jury. So he began his cross-examination in an
ordinary tone of voice, but with very great distinctness, like this : " I suppose — sir — I — must
— speak — very — loud — or — you — will — not
— hear — me." " Oh yes ! " answered the witness,
" I'm very deaf. You must speak very loud indeed,
or I shan't hear a word." The lawyer then lowered
his voice, but retained the same distinctness, till
he spoke only in a whisper, yet the witness heard
and answered without the least difficulty. At
length, turning to the jury, he said : " You can see
for yourselves how much credit is to be given to
this witness. He pretends to be very deaf, yet he
hears all my whispers." And but for the interfer-
ence of the judge, who saw that the honest old
man had not discriminated between *loudness* and
distinctness, the jury would have been deceived by
the lawyer's trick.

However useful Dr. Kirk may have been in Boston, it was a great loss to the churches in general
when he left the work of the evangelist for that of
the pastor.

HOW A MAN OVER EIGHTY YEARS OLD FOUND CHRIST.

N the month of October, 1876, the writer supplied an Orthodox church in a central and somewhat famous agricultural Massachusetts town for two Sabbaths. Entertainment was provided at the house of a prominent citizen, whose wife, a most godly woman, requested after the first Sunday service that I should visit her father, living at the other end of the considerable village.

I went with her to his residence, and found a man eighty-two years of age; hair white as snow; hearing considerably impaired; voice broken; form, once erect and commanding, now bent; his body more or less under the power of a disease that seemed to give to the mind power of perception in proportion as it took from the animal vitality. He had heard of my coming to the place, and of work which had been done in the village hard by the spring previous; and he immediately professed great thankfulness that I had called upon him.

Commencing talk at once upon the one subject, he told me that he felt himself near his earthly

end; that he had no hope; that he wanted, as he
thought above all things else, to become a Christian; but that he did not know how. I showed
him, as well as I was able, the successive steps that
lead from the plain of selfishness and sin up to the
foot of the cross, and asked him to do three things :
read the Bible; think upon this one subject, and
pray; and after prayer with him and for him, bade
him good-by.

The next Sunday I visited him again, and found
that the Holy Spirit had been doing His blessed
office-work in the old man's heart; that he saw
himself a great sinner against God; and the burden of his sorrow came from the fact that he had
lived until he had become a moss-covered monument of God's mercy, without ever having acknowledged the kindness of the King who had forbear-
ingly kept him; and his wail of agony was : "God
will not forgive me;" "God cannot forgive me;"
"Why have I abused His mercy?" "Why have I
wronged Him so long?"

I told him in slow simple words about Christ;
the old, old story; that He came from heaven to
earth to save *penitent* sinners, whether they had
sinned one year or eighty. But I could not make
him grasp even the possibility that he could be
saved; and after prayer, I left him, requesting that
he read every day some part of Christ's history, as
found in the New Testament, in addition to the
fifty-third chapter of Isaiah, and to pray constantly
for the blessing that in his heart he wanted.

Three weeks afterward I was called again to the same parish, and on Saturday night went to see the old man. He had come slowly to feel that there was hope for even him, but felt no relief from the burden he was constantly bearing. He said that he had sincerely and persistently sought forgiveness, and to show the sincerity of his desire to honor Christ, he wanted to unite with the church, so that all his neighbors might know of his new fealty. I told him he was not ready to do that, but there was one thing he could do that would honor God as well as test his willingness to obey Him; and that was to pray in his family. He immediately said that he never prayed aloud, and he could not; that he could not speak above a whisper anyway. I told him that God could hear a penitent whisper, and would, quicker than a presumptuous shouting; and, asking him to begin the new week rightly by praying with his waiting wife, I left him. The next evening I saw him again. His face had upon it not a look of despair, but of unutterable sadness. He said he saw clearly that it was his duty to do what had been suggested, but he could not bring himself to the doing; and he therefore felt that he might not be sincere in his purpose to serve God. I said to him that the morning of the golden Sabbath had passed, but could he not begin that night? and then found for him these passages: "Strive to enter in;" "the Kingdom of heaven suffereth violence, and the violent take it by force," and then left him to read and think.

Monday night, having concluded to remain in the parish during the week, I saw him again. And oh! the change in his face. The look of sorrow gone, and in its place the illumination of Christ's forgiving love! And then he told me, brokenly, the story, bowing for the first time in his life before God, and audibly asking for forgiveness, forgiveness, forgiveness! And then and there the sweet consciousness that the sins of fourscore years were washed away in the Saviour's atoning blood.

I saw him several times afterward; his soul all full of love and peace. Family worship was maintained; and he said he found his greatest blessing where he found his first sweet relief. He was soon examined for admission to the church and accepted, but increasing disease prevented him from making a public profession, and in less than three months the saved soul of the old man was with Christ in paradise. His death was peaceful — the hand of Jesus under his sinking head.

Three lessons the experience of this old man taught:

1. He frequently said, that he heard a sermon twenty years before, by whom and when delivered he could not tell, that had been more or less in his mind ever since; that he had had twenty years of a kind of conviction of sin, which at length ended in pardon and peace. Who that preacher was

eternity will reveal. But he was the means of awakening a feeling in that man's heart, that did not, would not, die! And for the comfort of honest, faithful toilers for the Master, it may be safely said, there are millions of just such cases.

2. We who work for Christ need patience. It took the clogged mind of the old man weeks to perceive what some can see at a glance ; and there may be young persons whose habits of thinking, or *not* thinking, put them where years had put this pilgrim.

3. Men are frequently willing to do duty tomorrow, who are unwilling to do duty today. The old man was willing to unite with the church the next month, but was unwilling to pray in his family the next minute. It is always, as in his case, *present* and not future obedience that secures the blessing.

CHRISTIAN WORK.

OPPORTUNITIES to do work for our Lord
lie all about us.   I was hastening past the
plate-glass show window where a young
man was closely observing some pictures.   " You
cannot stop," said the adversary who goes about to
devour; but " He who spake as never man spake,"
whispered, " Return."

Looking within as the stranger was doing, I
said : " Do you know where that paper is published? The type is clear and printing is well done
in these days."

" It is, and just coming from four years at sea I
know how to value books and papers."

" Four years at sea ?   You look young."

" Father died; mother with five children must
have help, and I entered the merchant service, sir,"
and a pure-faced, blue-eyed young man looked up
at me.

" Where have you sailed ? "

" Many times across the Atlantic to German,
French and Mediterranean ports, sir."

" Do you go back to sea ? "

" I never liked it. I'm now going to tell my

mother and sisters good-by, and start for Iowa to-morrow, sir."

" You've laid up some money ? "

" Not much. I sent what I could to mother and have now a few dollars for her, saving just enough for a second-class ticket to Iowa."

" It's difficult to save money at sea, isn't it ? "

" At boarding-houses we often have to advance money, and the ship pays, and sometimes we do not get the debt all paid up till the end of the voyage ; then wait a month before we can ship again."

" Most of the sailors drink, smoke and swear, do they not ? "

"Most of them smoke, but late years they do not drink and curse as much. I've been on two Christian ships, sir."

" What's a Christian ship ? "

" Meetings on Sunday, sometimes once a week, some good books to read, and kindness, sir."

" Some of your companions are Christians ? "

" Three or four have it in them, and it comes out, sir."

"What about *your* love to Him who died that you may live ? "

" Sometimes I feel that I'm forgiven, and then, I don't know how, can't understand and don't get on well, sir."

" Christ tells Nicodemus in the third chapter, and the woman at the well in the fourth, of John, just how to repent and come to Him."

"You on shore with Sundays, meetings, and things standing still, can do well; but at sea we are tossed and tumbled about, sir."

"*Look to Him!*" we said, grasping his rough sailor hand, as in tremulous tones, through tears, he answered: "How is it that you feel such an interest in a sailor boy, sir?"

The talk ended, and the young man went toward his western home, but who knows the effect produced upon that heart, which so warmed toward the Christian man who was interested in a stranger?

THE TRUE HEROIC.

HONORS to the heroic! not the blast
  Of trumpet for the warrior from the field ;
  But the sweet music heart and conscience yield
For duty done ; the glittering falchion cast
  In battle's furnace sheds a wondrous light,
  But not heroic ; 'tis the blinking sight
Of Harvest's sickle in the golden grain
Wielded by hearts that might have held the reign
  Of some great conquerer on his spot of earth
  If they had loved the sword ! They own true worth,
The true heroic ! At his humble plow
  Showed Cincinnatus real glory, not
  Red Alexander in his chariot ! lot
Sublime the Heroic ! stars are native to its brow.
. . . .

And not alone the giants of our race !
  But those that give their widow's mite, themselves
  To aid in trouble ! the swart slave who delves
In mines for wife and children ! those that face
  The deadly pestilence for others' weal ;
  The scissors-grinder with his lungs that steel
Powders with death ; the seamstress who works on
Through crawling midnight hours with cheek made wan
By wasting toil ! these show their starry hearts
  In trouble, and still strive when lesser souls,
  Gilded by fame or pleasure, find their goals
In earth's applause for deeds that own no darts
Of sacrifice or duty piercing through
The flowers, that fawning praise and bending flattery strew.

MARK, THE POOR MAN'S GOSPEL.

BIBLE societies are accustomed to print the gospels separately, for circulation in heathen countries. If we had the little books before us, we could not fail to perceive how inferior to the rest in bulk is the Gospel of Mark. We all remember its sixteen chapters, compared with the twenty-eight of Matthew, twenty-four of Luke, and twenty-one of John. Chapters, however, do not truly indicate extent of narrative, but pages do; and these have almost exactly the same proportion of numbers as the chapters themselves. It appears, then, that Mark's Gospel is little more than half as long as the two other synoptic narratives. Can we make any conjecture as to the reason in the divine mind for this disproportion?

The Gospels were written, we remember, on parchment, a costly material as compared with paper; and written not in such small letters as we now employ, but in far larger ones; which, therefore would require many skins to make a book of any length. Probably not more than forty verses, even if in double columns, could be written on a skin. The 673 verses of Mark would therefore require sixteen skins. These could not cost less, we may suppose, than a quarter of a dollar apiece; making four dollars' worth of parchment for the whole. Mark's Gospel in a Greek Testament contains not much less than 40,000 letters. If a scribe could make a thousand a day, with the care necessary in those square alphabets, it would take him nearly six weeks to copy this Gospel. If his wages were only fifty cents a day, they would amount to twenty dollars in that time. Thus we reach the conclusion that a copy of Mark, in that age, would be worth about twenty-five dollars, or its equivalent in money of that time. How large a proportion of the early Christians would be able to possess it? Much more difficult would it be to purchase a Gospel twice as long, even though copied on a cheaper material.

I suppose, then, that this Gospel was made so short that it might be cheaper, and also read in less time; so that a larger number of individuals, or of churches, might be able to possess the principal facts of our Saviour's history. It was a sort of primer of Gospel truth, meant for circulation, not indeed among the poor, but among those who were only moderately rich.

We might suppose that a writer influenced by such views, beside omitting the genealogy, the birth, the infancy, the temptation and the principal discourses of Christ, would choose for narration such events as were peculiarly salient and striking in his life. A special vividness of narrative does, indeed, appear in many of his recitals, suited to fix attention and abide in the memory.

In the account of the Gadarene demoniac, while the other Evangelists are content with saying that the unhappy man "abode in the tombs, without clothes, exceeding fierce," Mark proceeds to tell that "no man could bind him, no, not with chains; because that he had been often bound with fetters and chains, and the chains had been plucked asunder by him, and the fetters broken in pieces; neither could any man tame him. And always, night and day, he was in the mountains, and in the tombs, crying, and cutting himself with stones." Nothing can exceed this description in vividness and horror. Nothing could be better suited to take the attention of common people.

Very much the same is true in the narrative of the demoniac healed just after the transfiguration, which in Mark occupies twice the space given to it by the other Evangelists. Nor is this the languor of an inferior writer, since every line is full of graphic touches; seeming to say that the author's own mind was strangely excited by incidents of this kind.

We all know how much life is imparted to a tale by the mention of specific facts, which localize and vivify an occurrence. Such an effect is produced by Mark's mention of the "pillow in the hinder part of the ship," when Jesus slept in the storm on the lake; of the "green grass," on which the multitude were told to sit down, "company by company," "like leek beds;" and of the "executioner" (in Greek, speculator or spiculator), rather the "guardsman," or spearsman, or halberdier, sent to behead John the Baptist.

Short as this Gospel is, it is Mark alone who tells us of the blind man whom Jesus "took by the hand, and led him out of the town;" and of the young man who followed Jesus the night of his arrest, "having a linen cloth cast about his naked body;" who gives us the striking parable of the mustard seed; and who brings in the Syriac words, "Ephphatha," "Talitha cumi."

All these attractive touches are suited to a Gospel meant for common people, of whom almost all the world is made up. Not that these features unfit it in the least for superior minds; but the lower classes *must* be made sure of, because they are the majority. Mark was "sister's son to Barnabas," and lived in the great house in Jerusalem to which Peter directed his steps when liberated by the angel. He was accustomed therefore to good society. And yet, Peter calls him "Marcus, my son;" implying peculiar intimacy. The first act of Jesus, in his public life, as narrated by Mark, is the calling of Simon and Andrew from their occupation with the net; and the second miracle performed is the healing of Simon's wife's mother. Simon, the name his mother gave him, not Peter, is the name used for this Apostle at first by Mark. All these things seem to be indications of Peter's presence and agency in the preparation of this Gospel. The plebeian origin and character of Peter may therefore be assumed, in accordance with tradition, to have influenced the selection of points for narration, and these characteristic touches of manner. And surely none of the Apostles was more suitable as the quasi-author of a poor man's Gospel.

HOW AN ENGLISHMAN GETS BURIED.

NE of the things which impresses you strangely, is the fact that they think so much about it, and so long beforehand. There are societies innumerable, all over the land, whose members, workingmen, pay into their funds eighteen pence (about forty cents) a week ; and not least among the benefits thus secured, as they look at it, is the assurance of a decent and respectable burial when they die. A "workus funeral" is what they dread. Nor will you wonder when you have witnessed one. In an outer section of London I have seen hearse, coffin, pall, horse and driver, all having the work-house mark so deeply indented that it was a sickening sight. Two old women, in mean, work-house garb, probably nurses to the departed, were feebly following on foot. At a corner of the street a Punch and Judy show was performing. It was such a rare treat to the poor things, that they could not resist the temptation to linger and gaze, while the hearse moved on, leaving them to catch up as best they could.

But you will be very much more surprised if you follow up inquiries in this direction. We will

suppose you want to get buried yourself. Of course
you will have secured the place, and will have had
it put in perfect readiness beforehand.   That is to
say, you will have purchased your lot in a cemetery,
four feet by ten, more or less, probably less, unless
you happen to be a foreigner, in which case you
cannot be the holder of so much real estate in England until you shall have been made a British subject by a parliamentary act of naturalization, cost-
ing you five hundred pounds. This arranged, you
construct your grave, of brick and very deep, a
family grave or vertical tomb.   All is finished and
ready for use, being closed at the top and sealed
with covering of flat stone. In due time you come
to seek admission for yourself. You are met at
the threshold by an official who demands an
entrance fee of one guinea to ten guineas, or more,
according to your respectability, and the quality of
your grave. This is a perquisite of the company,
if the cemetery belongs to a company ; and of the
clergyman or minister, if the cemetery is an
appendage of a church or chapel. I believe a
guinea is the lowest sum demanded, though it be
for a child a day old.   And this charge is repeated
as often as the grave is opened to receive a new
inmate. It is the minister's fee for giving you
leave to open your own grave. This makes up
only a part of the very large income which often
accrues to the incumbent of a parish church from
the graveyard. Many of the interments are in

common graves ; that is to say, a very deep grave is opened, without bricks, and body after body is interred, from different families, a round fee being paid to the minister for each, until the graves can contain no more.

I have seen the coffin containing the remains of a most honored and beloved deacon of a Congregational church, with so shallow a covering of earth that great care was taken to keep it from the knowledge of the widow. And all those full graves are still the property of the church, and they have all been filled and emptied many times ; for just as fast as the remains are sufficiently "earth to earth, and dust to dust," they are taken out, and huddled into a common vault in a retired section of the ground. The cemetery in which the honored deacon was interred, is in the beautiful village of Wyke Regis, on the south coast, and is the appendage of a very fine old stone church, with a tower rising so high that it seems as a landmark to vessels at sea. The cemetery is enclosed by a wall of faced stone, about three feet high. As Wyke Regis is the ecclesiastical mother of the adjacent parish of Weymouth, a popular watering place, the interments have been very numerous for a succession of generations, and in this way, with the repeated emptying and refilling of the graves, the surface has been gradually raised till it is nearly even with the top of the wall. Thus there is a deep covering of rich mold, in which is a large admixture of human dust. The grass is very green, and has a tendency to so rank a growth that it requires frequent cropping down. I have often seen splendid Southdowns feeding there, and the thought would come of itself that it was a very possible thing for a man to dine off of his own grandfather.

I have said that you pay for the privilege of lying down in your own grave "one guinea to ten guineas, *or more.*" In the ground of which I have been speaking is a large vault, belonging to a family of wealth and high position, which has been many years absent from the place. After a long period, application was made to the rector of the parish, for permission to open it for the reception of a member of the family. Such permission was very cheerfully granted on payment of a fee of forty guineas. This was in strict accordance with the rule in such a case made and provided. And not so very extortionate, either, if you will consider it ; for that vault had brought no income to the rector for a long time ; whereas if the ground had been at liberty, there was room for several graves, which might have been filled and emptied more than once, perhaps, so realizing a total sum of more than forty guineas to the minister.

This same rector in the Established Church of England has the absolute right to decide what shall be the inscription on your tombstone. Neither does he hesitate to exercise this right, if so disposed. Not long since a little girl died and was buried by the parish church. The sorrowing father had a headstone prepared with the following inscription :

"In loving memory of Annie Augusta Keet, the youngest daughter of the Rev. H. Keet, Wesleyan minister; who died at Owston Ferry, May 11, 1874. 'Safe sheltered from the storms of life.'"

The Rev. G. E. Smith, vicar of the parish, forbade the bringing of the stone into the yard, unless "Rev." and "Wesleyan minister" were stricken out! Whereupon the father addressed the Bishop of Lincoln, in whose diocese these things are taking place, and received for answer that the vicar is not exceeding his proper powers. The Rev. Mr. Keet next seeks redress from the Archbishop of Canterbury, Primate of all England, who replies very kindly and courteously and cautiously; does not feel called on to give an opinion as to the legal question, but thinks the objection urged by the Rev. G. E. Smith ought not to be made, and will be surprised if the Bishop of Lincoln does not coincide with him. Back again to the Bishop of Lincoln goes the sorrowing father, to sue for permission to place the stone he has prepared over the grave of his dear child, and gets in reply an elaborate deliverance of the prelate, showing him that he is not "reverend," nor "a minister," in any sense which a Bishop of the Established

Church can recognize; and that to permit such a misstatement of facts to be engraven on stone within the consecrated precincts of a parochial burying ground, would be a grave dereliction on the part of bishop or vicar in the Church of England.

The case of the Rev. Henry Keet and his dead child is a sample of occurrences which are slowly, yet surely, working great changes in English ecclesiastical affairs. The practical lesson from all which is that, whatever other things we may need, we can do very well without a State church.

THE CHINESE IN CALIFORNIA.

E have seen Chinatown in San Francisco by day and by night ; above ground and below, and find that a host of calumnies in regard to the Mongolian working men and merchants are refuted by a close study of facts at first hand.

In a Chinese restaurant of the higher class, we sat down at a round table to fruit cakes, olives and several other kinds of dried fruits, and to very delicious tea. This was served without milk or sugar, and was made by placing the tea in the bottom of each individual's cup, and pouring over it boiling water. The tea itself is never allowed to boil. A saucer is inverted over the tea in each cup, and the liquid is turned out into a tiny cup for drinking.

Three Chinese gentlemen were in the company, and were certainly equal in manners to any of their companions. They were much amused at the gradual attainment, on our part, of triumph in the use of chop sticks. We were shown the kitchen in the restaurant, and the rooms for cheap meals, and were impressed with the neatness of the place and the variety of the food.

In nine cases out of ten, the average Chinese working men are cleanlily dressed. Their white stockings were, to us, a perpetual amazement. Over and over, we saw Mongolian laundrymen with baskets on their backs, and with singularly stainless white hose. The rafts on which a large portion of the river population of China live are often whitewashed, and so are the little huts of the poorer classes.

We visited several private houses in which we were received with cordiality, and where we found only neatness and thrift, although, in no case, a social position above that in which slatternliness is common enough among European emigrants. The homes we entered were those of Christian Chinese. In one of them we found a little babe, of whom the whole neighborhood, we were told, was particularly proud, although its rights as a native born American are few and uncertain.

Mr. Gibson, the foremost friend of the Chinese in San Francisco, was received with evident affection in all the Chinese homes, and especially among his scholars at the Methodist Chinese Mission House. This building has been preserved from incendiary fires only by the heroism of its occupants and the friendliness of all its immediate neighbors. We sat in Mr. Gibson's parlor, and felt that we were in the house of a hero who needs no better indorsement than the fact of his being burned in effigy and threatened with mobs by the

Kearneyite roughs, while he is universally beloved by all good men. Even the virulent anti-Chinese press in San Francisco, admits that his book on "The Chinese in America," is a candid and able discussion of its topic. Senator Morton was in entire agreement with Otis Gibson on the Chinese question ; and so, indeed, is the most efficient part of the whole church on the Pacific coast.

We visited the rooms of the six Chinese Companies, and noticed the ebony tea stands and chairs, the gilded mottoes and the long robe of one of the Presidents, to whom we were introduced. We were assured by the officers at these rooms that Chinese working men make no servile contracts with the companies, and that there are no coolies or serfs in California. The same assurance, which agrees entirely with Senator Morton's report, came to us from missionaries, lawyers, preachers, and all reputable quarters in San Francisco.

.   .   .   .

The Chinese question is really whether the monopoly of low-paid labor shall be given to the Irish and other foreign elements, or shall be divided with the Chinamen? If the Chinamen now in San Francisco were expelled, wages would go up again, not to the hight at which they stood in the gold period, but far higher than they are now. At present they are conspicuously higher

than they are in the East. There was a day in
California when the average working man was paid
ten dollars for ten hours of labor, and eggs cost
twenty-five cents apiece. The time has now come
when the Chinaman receives about what we pay
white laborers in the East.

John Chinaman has not displaced anybody. He
has filled up gaps. White men, let us suppose,
abandon a mine when it will not pay three dollars
a day to each laborer. In comes John Chinaman,
and is content with two dollars a day, and he works
the mine. Has he displaced the miner who aban-
dons the mine? He has taken his place, but he
has only filled up a vacancy.

If a man wishes to start a woolen factory, and
must pay three dollars a day for labor, he sees he
cannot do it in San Francisco and compete with
Lowell and Lawrence. In comes John Chinaman,
and can be hired for a price at which it will pay to
manufacture woolen goods on the Pacific slope.
The Irishman with the pick-axe and the hod does
part of the work of putting up the factory, and
there is work made in various ways for all the
higher grades of labor by the coming in of laborers
at prices that permit profit. The Pacific slope
needs diversification of labor, and the Chinaman
has helped supply this need. Wages will come to
a level on the Pacific slope, and manufacturing will
start up in California.

The fact that 100,000 Chinamen find constant

employment on the Pacific coast at a respectable rate of remuneration, is proof that they are needed there. A man who employs Chinamen is to be counted as in favor of Chinese immigration. If 140,000 votes should be cast against Chinese immigration in California, it would yet be true that the majority are really in favor of it, because more than 70,000 people in California employ Chinamen. The newspapers of San Francisco do not properly represent the feelings of the best classes of society there on the Chinese question.

Many people are of the opinion that we are in danger of a Mongolian deluge. When the sky falls we shall catch larks; but we do not see any danger of its falling, and do not want Congress to set traps for larks yet.

The most important query on the Chinese problem appears to be, not what is popular, but what is inevitable. We hold that it is inevitable that the Pacific slope will reach one third of the way around the globe for the teas and silks of China and Japan, rather than three quarters of the way around it in the other direction through England and India for the same things. We shall inevitably become the chief commercial rival of England in the immense trade of the Orient. It is inevitable that great commercial considerations will require that the treaties of the United States with China should secure, as they now do, to American citizens residing there, equal rights with those of any other foreigners residing there. International law and the public sentiment of the world will justify China in refusing to Americans in China the rights of the most favored nation there, if the United States refuse to the Chinese in America the rights of the most favored nation here. It is highly important for us to cultivate relations of peace with China, and to treat her in every respect with the same justice that we exercise in the case of other nations. Japan is growing in importance. The reforms there will be caught up in China ultimately. A not distant future will witness the introduction of railroads, and telegraphs, and newspapers, and schools, into Japan and China. The regeneration of Asia is a great event, approaching us with a tread which will produce reverberations long after present generations are forgotten, and which already causes tremor in the soil of the Pacific slope. We believe that it immensely concerns America to keep step with the colossal movement, for it is doubtless God's plan for the religious education of an empire that was old when Greece was young.

WHITE VIOLETS.

YEARS since, when first this little one —
This child, with color of the sun
Upon her head, and in her eyes
The glad, awakening surprise
Of senses new to all things sweet —
Had learned to walk, I taught her feet
To love the meadow ways that spread
Such a soft carpet to her tread.

One path we knew, where we could find
Beside the brook, and hidden behind
The tallest grasses, oh, such sweet
White violets!   Their shy retreat
Was cool and wet, even when the sun
Was high and hot; and every one
Her fingers plucked so lovingly
Seemed like her own pure self to me.

Who planted them, and made them grow,
Such crowds of them, she wished to know.
"God did it; He does everything,"
I said.   " He teaches birds to sing,
And shows them where to find their food;
He teaches children to be good;
He watches even these violets;
He never fails — never forgets!"

Later, we sought the self-same spot
For the sweet flowers, but found them not.
With ready eyes and eager face
She roamed about the favorite place.
Above us yellow orioles swung;
About us scores of bobolinks sung;
Until, at last, grown tired and hot,
I heard her sigh, "God *has* forgot!"

Just then, down by the water's side,
A large white cluster I espied,
Half covered in their cosy nook
With the long grasses of the brook.
Grieved that her baby faith was weak,
I pointed to them — did not speak.
She saw, and cried, as quick as thought,
In glad surprise, "God hasn't forgot!"

"START RIGHT."

THE other day I saw at a railroad station two
advertisements for some Western road, which
attracted my attention. The two differed only in
the color of the pasteboard. At the head of each
was a human hand, with the fore-finger outstretched,
pointing authoritatively. On the palm of the hand
was printed, in clear type, "Start Right."

But the deeper meaning! Those travelers on
that longer road! That fast express! The eternal
destinies! The many lurements enticing to the
wrong road! "Start Right;" yes, start right; and
having started right, hold on to the end.

"He watches even these violets."

Page 307.

WRITING DOWN THE BIBLE.

N one of the winter vacations of my college course, when I was teaching school in a rural district and "boarding around," I heard from the Christian people of the neighborhood many stories of an old man in one of the families who possessed a wonderful knowledge of the Bible. He could "quote it," the country folk said, "from beginning to end;" and he could explain it in a way that put to shame professional exegetes. The faith of this expounder of the Word was that of the "Univarsalers," as some of his neighbors expressed it; and orthodox disputants stood greatly in awe of him.

I confess that when, in that course of human events which makes up the life of a country schoolmaster, it became necessary for me to seek a shelter in the home inhabited by this venerable controversialist, I went with considerable trepidation. I was told that he would surely bring his batteries to bear upon my theology, and although I had studied the Bible from my childhood, I felt myself quite unable to cope with a veteran expositor of so great fame.

I was not misinformed concerning the readiness
of the old gentleman to engage in controversy.
He knew that I was studying for the ministry, and
a theological tussle with "the master" was therefore among the things decreed. No sooner was the
supper finished, and the cloth removed, than the
examination of the candidate was proceeded with.
At first I answered evasively, indicating my unwil-
lingness to be led into any dispute ; but before long
the old gentleman developed his own position,
and I began to listen with interest, and to question
him. The theological system thus discovered was
certainly a remarkable one. My philosopher and
prophet was, as I had been told, a Universalist ;
but the school to which he belonged was one of
which I have found no other representative. Briefly
stated, his theory was that the judgment and the
resurrection took place at the time of the destruction of Jerusalem ; that *then* "all nations " were
gathered together in Palestine, and that the
righteous were separated from the wicked as
the shepherd divideth his sheep from the goats ;
that the wicked then went away into everlasting
punishment, but the righteous into life eternal ;
and that since that day we are living in a gospel
age ; and all who are born are redeemed and saved
by the blood of Christ. Sinners who lived before
the judgment, that is to say, the destruction of
Jerusalem, are therefore now, and will be forever,
in endless misery ; salvation is universal only for

those who have lived since that day, and those who are to live hereafter.

Such was the theory, and as my aged inquisitor unfolded it, I began to be curious about its Scriptural foundations. Doubtless he must be resting this theory, which he so confidently broached, upon a wide induction of Scripture. I asked for his proofs, and he told me that there was a single passage which established his doctrine beyond all questioning. It was in the fifth chapter of John's Gospel, the twenty-eighth and twenty-ninth verses. Bringing me his old Bible, thumbed and yellow in the leaves which enclosed this text, he laid his finger upon it and asked me triumphantly whether that was not enough. I did not at once perceive the application, and he therefore proceeded with his exegesis :

" Marvel not at this : for the hour is coming in the which (' the ' was emphasized in his reading) all that are in their graves shall hear His voice and shall come forth ; they that have done good, unto the resurrection of life, and they that have done evil unto the resurrection of damnation."

" The hour is coming in *the ;* " said the good man. " That means ' in thy day.' He was talking to his disciples and the Jews. It was in *their* day, therefore, that the dead in their graves were to hear the voice of God and come forth — the good to the resurrection of life, and the evil to the resurrection of damnation. It was in *the*, that is in their generation, that the resurrection and the judgment were to occur. They did occur when 'all nations' were gathered at the destruction of Jerusalem. Therefore we are living after the judgment, and therefore there is no condemnation for us; but in Christ we are all made alive, and saved with an everlasting salvation."

After a few moments of silent admiration of this astonishing exegesis, I inquired whether there were any other texts confirming this view. He did not know of any, but asked if this one did not sufficiently prove it. Then I took the dictionary and showed him the difference between the article "the," and the pronoun "thee," explaining as well as I could the grammatical construction, and showing him that his text could not be read as he had read it, without making nonsense of it. The old gentleman was at first inclined to treat my suggestions with scorn; but he did at last consent to look at the dictionary, and at the difference between "the" and "thee" as I pointed them out to him in the Testament; and when at last I asked him whether he would not have thought it hard usage if, when he invited me to "walk into the house," I had interpreted "the" to mean "thy," and had taken possession, and endeavored to turn him out of doors, he began to get a glimpse of a distinction between the words which had never before dawned on him. But the revelation brought to the worthy man nothing but pain. He took his old Bible, and read over and over, in a dazed and dejected way, the familiar passage on which his whole theological system had rested, and finally shutting up the book with some emphasis, he laid it upon the table and said, half wrathfully and half grievingly: "Well, if that is so, I may just as well throw my Bible into the fire!"

How it fared with his theology after this I never knew; probably his confidence in the theory of which he had so long been the champion soon recovered from the shock which the dictionary gave it, and reënforced by a little will-power became stronger than ever. The faith of a lifetime is not often brushed aside by a mere orthographical discrepancy; and the man whose constructive genius is so large that he can build a theological system upon a particle of speech, is not a man to be daunted by the dictionary.

This little episode in my schoolmastering has always stood in my thought for an illustration of the fact that great reputations, as well as great theological systems, sometimes rest upon very slender foundations.

The good man's distress at finding his long unquestioned interpretation of a text so rudely challenged, was not, however, then, nor has it ever been, a mere matter of sport to me. I was sorry for his perplexity. I knew that he felt that I had personally injured him. The Bible was chiefly valuable to him because it contained that text; and

that text was precious to him because it seemed to
him to sustain a belief to which he had committed
all the energies of his soul; and my criticism was
threatening to take the very ground from under his
feet. No words could have expressed his feeling
but the words of the Psalmist: "If the foundations
be destroyed, what shall the righteous do?" And
no doubt he regarded these objections of mine to
his theory as a wanton assault upon the Bible
itself. It is always so. Question a man's exegesis,
and in nine cases out of ten he will denounce you
for attacking the Bible. Show him that by his
own blunders of spelling, or of syntax, he is reading a doctrine into the Sacred Word that never
was revealed by the Holy Ghost, and he will cry
out that you are " writing down the Bible." Such
is the egotism of dogmatism.

THE BABY'S DRESSES.

WE folded smooth the little dress,
    Creased with our darling's latest wear;
We set the tiny boots beside,
    Dear molds of feet so plump and fair;
We dropped a golden curl along
    The band that held it, wet with tears,
And left the silken sash a-knot,
    As ofttimes tied these last two years.
His "baby" pin still caught its folds,
    And half soiled sacque for chilly days
Filled heart and arms with longing ache,
    For all his winsome precious ways.
Ah! who shall say what vigils lone,
    Looking through tears, his mother holds
Above the garments, which, though gone,
    Hold still her baby in their folds!

We stood beside his *lovelier* dress —
    God's own fair garment given the boy,
Which, all his two sweet years on earth,
    Had been our never-failing joy.
We laid it 'mid the lily blooms
    Lining the casket waiting near,
And thought, "It is as white as they;
    'Sweets to the sweet,' most fitting here."
He needs this beauteous robe no more;
    And so we lay it safe away,
Its soft fair outlines rounded still
    By the dear spirit gone today.

HINDERING INQUIRERS.

WHEN I was a boy, there was a protracted meeting and a revival in our church. My parents talked and prayed with me, and at length I went into the inquiry-meeting under deep concern. I remember I sat leaning against a pillar in the pew, weeping. There had come to help our minister a neighboring pastor, widely known and honored then and now. Kneeling on the seat in front, he leaned over toward me kindly, and in a low voice talked long and earnestly with me. What he said was doubtless well said. But he who would guide an inquiring soul, with the Holy Spirit's aid, must first explain faith, and then help the soul to exercise it. This impulse toward Christ my friend was not giving me. He was holding me back by one strong, overpowering argument, from the course to which he urged me.

He did precisely the same thing, once again, years afterward, when also he was making a personal appeal to me, on another practical question; the only two instances in my life when he thus closely pressed me. I was a student in theology at Andover, on my way home in the cars, seated

next the window with a companion. The clergyman was passing through the cars, and, recognizing
me, came and knelt in the seat in front of me, and
leaning over toward me, in a low voice very kindly
urged me, when I left the seminary, to come back
and join the old Presbytery, where my father was
the oldest surviving Elder.

In both cases, his appeals were ineffectual. I
did not leave the Congregational church, and, what
is of far greater moment, it was not till years after
that fatal inquiry-meeting — years of weary wandering and of endless loss — that at last I came to
Christ. The delay was my own wicked act, no
doubt; but I often think, oh! if I had only begun
then, when my indifference was for once broken
up, what a gain it would have been! Why did
that good man, in that solemn hour, hinder the
soul he tried to aid?

I solemnly aver that the only thing of which I
was distinctly conscious, in either interview, was
the hot, steaming, reeking smell of *tobacco.* I was
helpless, overpowered. The church pillar would
not move, hard as I crowded back against it. The
car window would not open, furiously as I tugged
to lift it. And how near he was! And how long
he talked! And — I grow faint sometimes now at
the thought of my feelings then.

At family prayers this morning we read the thir-
tieth chapter of Exodus, and a little boy wanted to
know what was the good of his reading so carefully

about all those old candlesticks and lavers of the Jews. And so, after we were through, I preached a little sermon about the " sweet spices," and the " laver " " for Aaron and his sons, to wash with water, that they die not, when they come near to the altar to minister, a statute forever to him and his seed throughout their generations." A good text for such sermons is the divine command : " Be ye clean that bear the vessels of the Lord."

Yet let us have no bigotry on this subject. It was hardly a wise thing to do when a member of a leading church in a certain city vehemently opposed, and perhaps was the means of defeating, a motion to call one of our best preachers, because that preacher in so far failed to " eschew evil " as to chew evil weeds ; albeit, they say, he was found one Saturday night, years ago, in a town where no tobacco was sold, and had to drive eight miles to get his Sunday's supply; for that distinguished preacher and his excellent wife, being duly sworn, depose and say that tobacco abates tendencies to alarming disease, and after many banishments is esteemed a welcome friend. It is unfortunate for a minister to be thus dependent on a weed, just as it was unfortunate for Christmas Evans that he had lost one eye, and as it is for Milburn that he has lost both.

A father once had hopes that his son was about to commence a Christian life. He had persuaded him to give up the habit of smoking, which he had

brought home from California, and on sending him
to a neighboring city to live, gave him a letter of
introduction to his friend, a pastor of rare powers
and of great success, whom he hoped would fan
the feeble flame, and bring the boy to Christ.
"Father," wrote the son, "I like the doctor first-
rate. He knows the flavor of a good Havana.
When I called with your letter, he came to the
door with a cigar in his mouth, and asked me in,
and we had a good smoke." I happened to see
that father's countenance fall, and think now he
had good ground for his grief and pain.

Yet that eminent clergyman is more unfortunate than wrong, for he says: "I believe I am
'approved' in the use of tobacco. I use it purely
and religiously as a specific, not as a luxury, and
very moderately; for all the comfort of it as an
indulgence, I would not carry the aroma of it one
day; it has relieved me of miseries which almost
drove me wild." But when we received that boy
into the church years afterward, he said he had not
looked at tobacco since he gave his heart to Christ;
and would as soon think it right to maim his right
hand as to touch it again. There came with him
another young man — both had been rather wild in
the army — who could see nothing wrong in the
habit. He soon ran away from his widowed mother
in disgrace, and I never heard of him again; while
the one who had a conscience about tobacco is a
hard-working and useful home missionary to-day.

"Do you smoke, sir?" I was asked by a Christian lady in a pastoral call, who was inquiring how to gain religious influence on her husband's mind. "I do not," I replied. "Oh, I was in hopes you did!" she exclaimed. "My husband has a friend in ——, and his pastor (naming a minister I heartily esteem) used to come in evenings, and smoke and play cards with him, and he gained a great influence over him, and finally got him to join the church. I was thinking perhaps I could manage that way with my husband." I had to confess I never smoked a cigar in my life, and never learned even the names of the cards. My parents had given me the best advantages they could, but that part of a preparation for the ministry, in my case, had been left out.

In one of our prayer-meetings, the subject of questionable indulgences happened once to come up, and a young Scotch brother, now a successful New England pastor, rose and made a very short speech. "I always used to smoke," said he; "but when I was converted, the text, 'Happy is he that condemneth not himself in that thing which he alloweth,' put my pipe out, and it has not been lighted since."

www.ingramcontent.com/pod-product-compliance
Lightning Source LLC
Chambersburg PA
CBHW031727280326
41926CB00098B/633